Island of the Blue Dolphins

and Related Readings

McDougal Littell
A HOUGHTON MIFFLIN COMPANY
Evanston, Illinois • Boston • Dallas

Acknowledgments

Houghton Mifflin Company: *Island of the Blue Dolphins* by Scott
O'Dell. Copyright © 1960 by Scott O'Dell. Reprinted by permission of
Houghton Mifflin Company. All rights reserved.

Georgiana Valoyce-Sanchez: "The Dolphin Walking Stick" by
Georgiana Valoyce-Sanchez, from *The Sound of Rattles and Clappers*,
edited by Greg Sarris (The University of Arizona Press, 1994). Reprinted
by permission of the author.

Sierra Club Books and Douglas & McIntyre: Excerpt from *The World
of the Sea Otter* by Stefani Paine. Text copyright © 1993 by Stefani
Paine. Reprinted with the permission of Sierra Club Books and
Greystone Books/Douglas & McIntyre.

Holy Cow! Press: "The Ice-Hearts," from *Turtle Meat and Other
Stories* by Joseph Bruchac. Text copyright © 1992 by Joseph Bruchac.
Reprinted by permission of Holy Cow! Press, Duluth.

Dudley Randall: "Courage," from *More to Remember* by Dudley
Randall. Reprinted by permission of the author.

Kodansha International Ltd.: Excerpt from *The Girl with the White
Flag* by Tomiko Higa, translated by Dorothy Britton. Published by
Kodansha International Ltd. Copyright © 1991 by Kodansha
International Ltd. Reprinted by permission. All rights reserved.

Continued on page 194

Cover illustration by Nobee Kanayama.
Background photograph Copyright © 1993
Sense Interactive Corporation.

2002 Impression.

Printed in China

ISBN-13: 978-0-395-87473-8
ISBN-10: 0-395-87473-4

11 12 13 DSC 09 08

Contents

Island of the Blue Dolphins

Scott O'Dell

For
The Russell Children
Isaac
Dorsa
Clare
Gillian
and
Felicity
and to
Eric
Cherie
and
Twinkle

Chapter 1

I remember the day the Aleut ship came to our island. At first it seemed like a small shell afloat on the sea. Then it grew larger and was a gull with folded wings. At last in the rising sun it became what it really was— a red ship with two red sails.

My brother and I had gone to the head of a canyon that winds down to a little harbor which is called Coral Cove. We had gone to gather roots that grow there in the spring.

My brother Ramo was only a little boy half my age, which was twelve. He was small for one who had lived so many suns and moons, but quick as a cricket. Also foolish as a cricket when he was excited. For this reason and because I wanted him to help me gather roots and not go running off, I said nothing about the shell I saw or the gull with folded wings.

I went on digging in the brush with my pointed stick as though nothing at all were happening on the sea. Even when I knew for sure that the gull was a ship with two red sails.

But Ramo's eyes missed little in the world. They were black like a lizard's and very large and, like the eyes of a lizard, could sometimes look sleepy. This was the time when they saw the most. This was the way they looked now. They were half-closed, like those of a lizard lying on a rock about to flick out its tongue to catch a fly.

"The sea is smooth," Ramo said. "It is a flat stone without any scratches."

My brother liked to pretend that one thing was another.

"The sea is not a stone without scratches," I said. "It is water and no waves."

"To me it is a blue stone," he said. "And far away on the edge of it is a small cloud which sits on the stone."

"Clouds do not sit on stones. On blue ones or black ones or any kind of stones."

"This one does."

"Not on the sea," I said. "Dolphins sit there, and gulls, and cormorants, and otter, and whales too, but not clouds."

"It is a whale, maybe."

Ramo was standing on one foot and then the other, watching the ship coming, which he did not know was a ship because he had never seen one. I had never seen one either, but I knew how they looked because I had been told.

"While you gaze at the sea," I said, "I dig roots. And it is I who will eat them and you who will not."

Ramo began to punch at the earth with his stick, but as the ship came closer, its sails showing red through the morning mist, he kept watching it, acting all the time as if he were not.

"Have you ever seen a red whale?" he asked.

"Yes," I said, though I never had.

"Those I have seen are gray."

"You are very young and have not seen everything that swims in the world."

Ramo picked up a root and was about to drop it into the basket. Suddenly his mouth opened wide and then closed again.

"A canoe!" he cried. "A great one, bigger than all of our canoes together. And red!"

A canoe or a ship, it did not matter to Ramo. In the very next breath he tossed the root in the air and was gone, crashing through the brush, shouting as he went.

I kept on gathering roots, but my hands trembled as I dug in the earth, for I was more excited than my brother. I knew that it was a ship there on the sea and not a big canoe, and that a ship could mean many things. I wanted to drop the stick and run too, but I went on digging roots because they were needed in the village.

By the time I filled the basket, the Aleut ship had sailed around the wide kelp bed that encloses our island and between the two rocks that guard Coral Cove. Word of its coming had already reached the village of Ghalas-at. Carrying their weapons, our men sped along the trail which winds down to the shore. Our women were gathering at the edge of the mesa.

I made my way through the heavy brush and, moving swiftly, down the ravine until I came to the sea cliffs. There I crouched on my hands and knees. Below me lay the cove. The tide was out and the sun shone on the white sand of the beach. Half the men from our village stood at the water's edge. The rest were concealed among the rocks at the foot of the trail, ready to attack the intruders should they prove unfriendly.

As I crouched there in the toyon bushes, trying not to fall over the cliff, trying to keep myself hidden and yet to see and hear what went on below me, a boat left the ship. Six men with long oars were rowing. Their faces were broad, and shining dark hair fell over their eyes. When they came closer I saw that they had bone ornaments thrust through their noses.

Behind them in the boat stood a tall man with a yellow beard. I had never seen a Russian before, but my father had told me about them, and I wondered, seeing the way he stood with his feet set apart and his fists on his hips and looked at the little harbor as though it already belonged to him, if he were one of those men from the north whom our people feared. I was certain of it when the boat slid in to the shore and he jumped out, shouting as he did so.

His voice echoed against the rock walls of the cove. The words were strange, unlike any I had ever heard. Slowly then he spoke in our tongue.

"I come in peace and wish to parley," he said to the men on the shore.

None of them answered, but my father, who was one of those hidden among the rocks, came forward down the sloping beach. He thrust his spear into the sand.

"I am the Chief of Ghalas-at," he said. "My name is Chief Chowig."

I was surprised that he gave his real name to a stranger. Everyone in our tribe had two names, the real one which was secret and was seldom used, and one which was common, for if people use your secret name it becomes worn out and loses its magic. Thus I was known as Won-a-pa-lei, which means The Girl with the Long Black Hair, though my secret name is Karana. My father's secret name was Chowig. Why he gave it to a stranger I do not know.

The Russian smiled and held up his hand, calling himself Captain Orlov. My father also held up his hand. I could not see his face, but I doubted that he smiled in return.

"I have come with forty of my men," said the

Russian. "We come to hunt sea otter. We wish to camp on your island while we are hunting."

My father said nothing. He was a tall man, though not so tall as Captain Orlov, and he stood with his bare shoulders thrown back, thinking about what the Russian had said. He was in no hurry to reply because the Aleuts had come before to hunt otter. That was long in the past, but my father still remembered them.

"You remember another hunt," Captain Orlov said when my father was silent. "I have heard of it, too. It was led by Captain Mitriff who was a fool and is now dead. The trouble arose because you and your tribe did all of the hunting."

"We hunted," said my father, "but the one you call a fool wished us to hunt from one moon to the next, never ceasing."

"This time you will need to do nothing," Captain Orlov said. "My men will hunt and we will divide the catch. One part for you, to be paid in goods, and two parts for us."

"The parts must be equal," my father said.

Captain Orlov gazed off toward the sea. "We can talk of that later when my supplies are safe ashore," he replied.

The morning was fair with little wind, yet it was the season of the year when storms could be looked for, so I understood why the Russian wished to move onto our island.

"It is better to agree now," said my father.

Captain Orlov took two long steps away from my father, then turned and faced him. "One part to you is fair since the work is ours and ours the risk."

My father shook his head.

The Russian grasped his beard. "Since the sea is

not yours, why do I have to give you any part?"

"The sea which surrounds the Island of the Blue Dolphins belongs to us," answered my father.

He spoke softly as he did when he was angry.

"From here to the coast of Santa Barbara—twenty leagues away?"

"No, only that which touches the island and where the otter live."

Captain Orlov made a sound in his throat. He looked at our men standing on the beach and toward those who had now come from behind the rocks. He looked at my father and shrugged his shoulders. Suddenly he smiled, showing his long teeth.

"The parts shall be equal," he said.

He said more, but I did not hear it, for at that instant in my great excitement I moved a small rock, which clattered down the cliff and fell at his feet. Everyone on the beach looked up. Silently I left the toyon bushes and ran without stopping until I reached the mesa.

Chapter 2

Captain Orlov and his Aleut hunters moved to the island that morning, making many trips from their ship to the beach of Coral Cove. Since the beach was small and almost flooded when the tide was in, he asked if he could camp on higher ground. This my father agreed to.

Perhaps I should tell you about our island so you will know how it looks and where our village was and where the Aleuts camped for most of the summer.

Our island is two leagues long and one league wide, and if you were standing on one of the hills that rise in the middle of it, you would think that it looked like a fish. Like a dolphin lying on its side, with its tail pointing toward the sunrise, its nose pointing to the sunset, and its fins making reefs and the rocky ledges along the shore. Whether someone did stand there on the low hills in the days when the earth was new and, because of its shape, called it the Island of the Blue Dolphins, I do not know. Many dolphins live in our seas and it may be from them that the name came. But one way or another, this is what the island was called.

The first thing you would notice about our island, I think, is the wind. It blows almost every day, sometimes from the northwest and sometimes from the east, once in a long while out of the south. All the winds except the one from the south are strong, and because of them the hills are polished smooth and the trees are small and twisted, even in the canyon that runs down to Coral Cove.

The village of Ghalas-at lay east of the hills on a small mesa, near Coral Cove and a good spring. About a half league to the north is another spring and it was there that the Aleuts put up their tents which were made of skins and were so low to the earth that the men had to crawl into them on their stomachs. At dusk we could see the glow of their fires.

That night my father warned everyone in the village of Ghalas-at against visiting the camp.

"The Aleuts come from a country far to the north," he said. "Their ways are not ours nor is their language. They have come to take otter and to give us our share in many goods which they have and which we can use. In this way shall we profit. But we shall not profit if we try to befriend them. They are people who do not understand friendship. They are not those who were here before, but they are people of the same tribe that caused trouble many years ago."

My father's words were obeyed. We did not go to the Aleut camp and they did not come to our village. But this is not to say that we did not know what they did—what they ate and in what way they cooked it, how many otter were killed each day, and other things as well—for someone was always watching from the cliffs while they were hunting, or from the ravine when they were in camp.

Ramo, for instance, brought news about Captain Orlov.

"In the morning when he crawls out of his tent he sits on a rock and combs until the beard shines like a cormorant's wing," Ramo said.

My sister Ulape, who was two years older than I, gathered the most curious news of all. She swore that there was an Aleut girl among the hunters.

"She is dressed in skins just like the men," Ulape said. "But she wears a fur cap and under the cap she has thick hair that falls to her waist."

No one believed Ulape. Everyone laughed at the idea that hunters would bother to bring their wives with them.

The Aleuts also watched our village, otherwise they would not have known about the good fortune which befell us soon after they came.

It happened in this way. Early spring is a poor season for fishing. The heavy seas and winds of winter drive the fish into deep water where they stay until the weather is settled and where they are hard to catch. During this time the village eats sparingly, mostly from stores of seeds harvested in autumn.

Word of our good fortune came on a stormy afternoon, brought by Ulape, who was never idle. She had gone to a ledge on the eastern part of the island hoping to gather shellfish. She was climbing a cliff on the way home when she heard a loud noise behind her.

At first she did not see what had caused the noise. She thought that it was the wind echoing through one of the caves and was about to leave when she noticed silvery shapes on the floor of the cove. The shapes moved and she saw that it was a school of large white bass, each one as big as she was. Pursued by killer whales, which prey upon them when seals are not to be found, the bass had tried to escape by swimming toward shore. But in their terror they had mistaken the depth of the water and had been tossed onto the rocky ledge.

Ulape dropped her basket of shellfish and set out for the village, arriving there so out of breath that she could only point in the direction of the shore. The women were cooking supper but all of them stopped and gathered around her, waiting for her to speak.

"A school of white bass," she finally said.

"Where? Where?" everyone asked.

"On the rocks. A dozen of them. Perhaps more than a dozen."

Before Ulape had finished speaking, we were running toward the shore, hoping that we would get there in time, that the fish had not flopped back into the sea, or that a chance wave had not washed them away.

We came to the cliff and looked down. The school of white bass was still on the ledge, glistening in the sun. But since the tide was high and the biggest waves were already lapping at the fish, there was no time to lose. One by one we hauled them out of reach of the tide. Then, two women carrying a single fish, for they were all of about the same size and heavy, we lifted them up the cliff and brought them home.

There were enough for everyone in our tribe for supper that night and the next, but in the morning two Aleuts came to the village and asked to speak to my father.

"You have fish," one of them said.

"Enough only for my people," my father answered.

"You have fourteen fish," the Aleut said.

"Seven now because we ate seven."

"From seven you can spare two."

"There are forty in your camp," my father replied, "and more than that of us. Besides, you have your own fish, the dried ones that you brought."

"We tire of that kind," the Aleut said.

He was a short man who only came to my father's

shoulders, and he had small eyes like black pebbles and a mouth like the edge of a stone knife. The other Aleut looked very much like him.

"You are hunters," my father said. "Go and hunt your own fish if you are tired of what you are now eating. I have my people to think of."

"Captain Orlov will hear that you refuse to share the fish."

"Yes, tell him," my father said. "But also why we refuse."

The Aleut grunted to his companion and the two of them stalked off on their short legs across the sand dunes that lay between the village and their camp.

We ate the rest of the white bass that night and there was much rejoicing. But little did we know, as we ate and sang and the older men told stories around the fire, that our good fortune would soon bring trouble to Ghalas-at.

Chapter 3

The wide beds of kelp which surround our island on three sides come close to the shore and spread out to sea for a distance of a league. In these deep beds, even on days of heavy winds, the Aleuts hunted. They left the shore at dawn in their skin canoes and did not return until night, towing after them the slain otter.

The sea otter, when it is swimming, looks like a seal, but is really very different. It has a shorter nose than a seal, small webbed feet instead of flippers, and fur that is thicker and much more beautiful. It is also different in other ways. The otter likes to lie on its back in the kelp beds, floating up and down to the motion of the waves, sunning itself or sleeping. They are the most playful animals in the sea.

It was these creatures that the Aleuts hunted for their pelts.

From the cliff I could see the skin canoes darting here and there over the kelp beds, barely skimming the water, and the long spears flying like arrows. At dark the hunters brought their catch into Coral Cove, and there on the beach the animals were skinned and fleshed. Two men, who also sharpened the spears, did this work, laboring far into the night by the light of seaweed fires. In the morning the beach would be strewn with carcasses, and the waves red with blood.

Many of our tribe went to the cliff each night to count the number killed during the day. They counted the dead otter and thought of the beads and other things that each pelt meant. But I never went to the cove and whenever I saw the hunters with their long spears skimming over the water, I was angry, for these animals were my friends. It was fun to see them playing or sunning themselves among the kelp. It was more fun than the thought of beads to wear around my neck.

This I told my father one morning.

"There are scarcely a dozen left in the beds around Coral Cove," I said. "Before the Aleuts came there were many."

"Many still live in other places around the island," he replied, laughing at my foolishness. "When the hunters leave they will come back."

"There will be none left," I said. "The hunters will kill them all. This morning they hunt on the south. Next week they move to another place."

"The ship is filled with pelts. In another week the Aleuts will be ready to go."

I was sure that my father thought they would leave soon, for two days before he had sent some of our young men to the beach to build a canoe from a log which had drifted in from the sea.

There are no trees on the island except the small ones stunted by the wind. When a log came ashore, as happened once in a long time, it was always carried to the village and worked on where a chance wave could not wash it away. That the men were sent to hollow out the log in the cove, and to sleep beside it during the night, meant that they were there to watch the Aleuts, to give the alarm should Captain Orlov try to sail off without paying us for the otter skins.

Everyone was afraid he might, so besides the men in the cove who watched the Aleut ship, others kept watch on the camp.

Every hour someone brought news. Ulape said that the Aleut woman spent a whole afternoon cleaning her skin aprons, which she had not done before while she had been there. Early one morning, Ramo said he had just seen Captain Orlov carefully trimming his beard so that it looked the way it did when he first came. The Aleuts who sharpened the long spears stopped this work and gave all their time to skinning the otter which were brought in at dusk.

We in the village of Ghalas-at knew that Captain Orlov and his hunters were getting ready to leave the island. Would he pay us for the otter he had slain or would he try to sneak away in the night? Would our men have to fight for our rightful share?

These questions everyone asked while the Aleuts went about their preparations—everyone except my father, who said nothing, but each night worked on the new spear he was making.

Chapter 4

The Aleuts left on a sunless day. Out of the north deep waves rolled down upon the island. They broke against the rocks and roared into the caves, sending up white sprays of water. Before night a storm would certainly strike.

Not long after dawn the Aleuts took down their skin tents and carried them to the beach.

Captain Orlov had not paid my father for the otter he had killed. So when the news came that the hunters had packed their tents, all of our tribe left the village and hurried toward Coral Cove. The men with their weapons went first and the women followed. The men took the trail that led to the beach, but the women hid themselves among the brush on the cliff.

Ulape and I went together far out on the ledge where I had hidden before when the hunters first came.

The tide was low and the rocks and the narrow beach were scattered with bundles of otter pelts. Half of the hunters were on the ship. The rest were wading into the water, tossing the pelts into a boat. The Aleuts laughed while they worked, as if they were happy to leave the island.

My father was talking to Captain Orlov. I could not hear their words because of the noise the hunters made, but from the way my father shook his head, I knew that he was not pleased.

"He is angry," Ulape whispered.

"Not yet," I said. "When he's really angry, he pulls his ear."

The men who were working on the canoe had stopped and were watching my father and Captain Orlov. The other men of our tribe stood at the foot of the trail.

The boat went off to the ship filled with otter. As it reached the ship, Captain Orlov raised his hand and gave a signal. When the boat came back it held a black chest which two of the hunters carried to the beach.

Captain Orlov raised the lid and pulled out several necklaces. There was little light in the sky, yet the beads sparkled as he turned them this way and that. Beside me, Ulape drew in her breath in excitement, and I could hear cries of delight from the women hidden in the brush.

But the cries suddenly ceased as my father shook his head and turned his back on the chest. The Aleuts stood silent. Our men left their places at the foot of the trail and moved forward a few steps and waited, watching my father.

"One string of beads for one otter pelt is not our bargain," my father said.

"One string and one iron spearhead," said Captain Orlov, lifting two fingers.

"The chest does not hold that much," my father answered.

"There are more chests on the ship," said the Russian.

"Then bring them to the shore," my father said. "You have one hundred and five bales of otter on the ship. There are fifteen here in the cove. You will need three more chests of this size."

Captain Orlov said something to his Aleuts that I

could not understand, but its meaning was soon clear. There were many hunters in the cove and as soon as he spoke they began to carry the otter pelts to the boat.

Beside me Ulape was scarcely breathing. "Do you think that he will give us the other chests?" she whispered.

"I do not trust him."

"When he gets the pelts to the ship he may leave."

"It is possible."

The hunters had to pass my father to reach the boat, and when the first one approached him, he stepped in his path.

"The rest of the pelts must stay here," he said, facing Captain Orlov, "until the chests are brought."

The Russian drew himself up stiffly and pointed to the clouds that were blowing in toward the island.

"I load the ship before the storm arrives," he said.

"Give us the other chests. Then I will help you with our canoes," my father replied.

Captain Orlov was silent. His gaze moved slowly around the cove. He looked at our men standing on the ledge of rock a dozen paces away. He looked upward toward the cliff and back at my father. Then he spoke to his Aleuts.

I do not know what happened first, whether it was my father who raised his hand against the hunter whose path he barred, whether it was this man who stepped forward with a bale of pelts on his back and shoved my father aside. It all happened so quickly that I could not tell one act from the other. But as I jumped to my feet and Ulape screamed and other cries sounded along the cliff, I saw a figure lying on the rocks. It was my father and blood was on his face. Slowly he got to his feet.

With their spears raised our men rushed down across the ledge. A puff of white smoke came from the deck of the ship. A loud noise echoed against the cliff. Five of our warriors fell and lay quiet.

Ulape screamed again and flung a rock into the cove. It fell harmlessly beside Captain Orlov. Rocks showered into the cove from many places along the cliff, striking several of the hunters. Then our warriors rushed in upon them and it was hard to tell one from the other.

Ulape and I stood on the cliff, and watched helplessly, afraid to use the rocks we held lest we injure our own men.

The Aleuts had dropped the bales of otter. They drew knives from their belts and as our warriors rushed upon them the two lines surged back and forth along the beach. Men fell to the sand and rose to fight again. Others fell and did not get up. My father was one of these.

For a long time it seemed that we would win the battle. But Captain Orlov, who had rowed off to the ship when the battle started, returned with more of his Aleuts.

Our warriors were forced backward to the cliffs. There were few of them left, yet they fought at the foot of the trail and would not retreat.

The wind began to blow. Suddenly Captain Orlov and his Aleuts turned and ran to the boat. Our men did not pursue them. The hunters reached the ship, the red sails went up, and the ship moved slowly between the two rocks that guard the cove.

Once more before it disappeared a white puff of smoke rose from the deck. As Ulape and I ran along the cliff a whirring sound like a great bird in flight passed above our heads.

The storm struck us as we ran, driving rain into our faces. Then other women were running beside us and their cries were louder than the wind. At the bottom of the trail we came upon our warriors. Many had fought on the beach. Few had left it and of these all were wounded.

My father lay on the beach and the waves were already washing over him. Looking at his body I knew he should not have told Captain Orlov his secret name, and back in our village all the weeping women and the sad men agreed that this had so weakened him that he had not lived through the fight with the Aleuts and the dishonest Russian.

Chapter 5

That night was the most terrible time in all the memory of Ghalas-at. When the fateful day had dawned the tribe numbered forty-two men, counting those who were too old to fight. When night came and the women had carried back to the village those who had died on the beach of Coral Cove, there remained only fifteen. Of these, seven were old men.

There was no woman who had not lost a father or a husband, a brother or a son.

The storm lasted two days and the third day we buried our dead on the south headland. The Aleuts who had fallen on the beach, we burned.

For many days after that the village was quiet. People went out only to gather food and came back to eat in silence. Some wished to leave and go in their canoes to the island called Santa Catalina, which lies far off to the east, but others said that there was little water on that island. In the end a council was held and it was decided to stay at Ghalas-at.

The council also chose a new chief to take my father's place. His name was Kimki. He was very old, but he had been a good man in his youth and a good hunter. The night he was chosen to be chief, he called everyone together, saying:

"Most of those who snared fowl and found fish in the deep water and built canoes are gone. The women, who were never asked to do more than stay at home, cook food, and make clothing, now must take the place of the men and face the dangers which abound beyond the village. There will be grumbling in Ghalas-at because of this. There will be shirkers. These will be punished, for without the help of all, all must perish."

Kimki portioned work for each one in the tribe, giving Ulape and me the task of gathering abalones. This shellfish grew on the rocks along the shore and was plentiful. We gathered them at low tide in baskets and carried them to the mesa where we cut the dark red flesh from the shell and placed it on flat rocks to dry in the sun.

Ramo had the task of keeping the abalones safe from the gulls and especially the wild dogs. Dozens of our animals, which had left the village when their owners had died, joined the wild pack that roamed the island. They soon grew as fierce as the wild ones and only came back to the village to steal food. Each day toward evening Ulape and I helped Ramo put the abalones in baskets and carry them to the village for safekeeping.

During this time other women were gathering the scarlet apples that grow on the cactus bushes and are called tunas. Fish were caught and many birds were netted. So hard did the women work that we really fared better than before when the hunting was done by the men.

Life in the village should have been peaceful, but it was not. The men said that the women had taken the tasks that rightfully were theirs and now that they had become hunters the men looked down upon them. There was much trouble over this until Kimki decreed that the work would again be divided—henceforth the men would hunt and the women harvest. Since there was already ample food to last through the winter, it no longer mattered who hunted.

But this was not the real reason why autumn and winter were unpeaceful in Ghalas-at. Those who had died at Coral Cove were still with us. Everywhere we went on the island or on the sea, whether we were fishing or eating or sitting by the fires at night, they were with us. We all remembered someone and I remembered my father, so tall and strong and kind. A few years ago my mother had died and since then Ulape and I had tried to do the tasks she had done, Ulape even more than I, being older. Now that my father was gone, it was not easy to look after Ramo, who was always into some mischief.

It was the same in the other houses of Ghalas-at, but more than the burdens which had fallen upon us all, it was the memory of those who had gone that burdened our hearts.

After food had been stored in autumn and the baskets were full in every house, there was more time to think about them, so that a sort of sickness came over the village and people sat and did not speak, nor ever laughed.

In the spring, Kimki called the tribe together. He had been thinking, he said, during the winter and had decided that he would take a canoe and go to the east to a country which was there and which he had once been to when he was a boy. It lay many days across the sea, but he would go there and make a place for us. He would go alone, because he could not spare more of our men for the voyage, and he would return.

The day that Kimki left was fair. We all went to the cove and watched him launch the big canoe. It held two baskets of water and enough tunas and dried abalone to last many days.

We watched while Kimki paddled through the

narrow opening in the rocks. Slowly he went through the kelp beds and into the sea. There he waved to us and we waved back. The rising sun made a silver trail across the water. Along this trail he disappeared into the east.

The rest of the day we talked about the journey. Would Kimki ever reach this far country about which nothing was known? Would he come back before the winter was over? Or never?

That night we sat around the fire and talked while the wind blew and the waves crashed against the shore.

Chapter 6

After Kimki had been gone one moon, we began to watch for his return. Every day someone went to the cliff to scan the sea. Even on stormy days we went, and on days when fog shrouded the island. During the day there was always a watcher on the cliff and each night as we sat around our fires we wondered if the next sun would bring him home.

But the spring came and left and the sea was empty. Kimki did not return!

There were few storms that winter and rain was light and ended early. This meant that we would need to be careful of water. In the old days the springs sometimes ran low and no one worried, but now everything seemed to cause alarm. Many were afraid that we would die of thirst.

"There are other things more important to ponder," said Matasaip, who had taken Kimki's place.

Matasaip meant the Aleuts, for it was now the time of year when they had come before. Watchers on the cliff began to look for the red sails and a meeting was held to plan what to do if the Aleuts came. We lacked the men to keep them from landing or to save our lives if they attacked us, which we were certain they would. Plans were therefore made to flee as soon as their ship was sighted.

Food and water were stored in canoes and these were hidden on the rocks at the south end of the island. The cliffs were steep here and very high, but we wove a stout rope of bull kelp and fastened it to rocks at the top of the cliff so that it hung to the water. As soon as the Aleut ship was sighted we would all go to the cliff and let ourselves down, one at a time. We would then leave in our canoes for the island of Santa Catalina.

Although the entrance to Coral Cove was too narrow for a ship to pass through safely at night, men were sent there to watch the cove from dusk to dawn, besides those who watched during the day.

Shortly afterwards, on a night of fine moon, one of the men came running back to the village. Everyone was asleep, but his cries quickly awakened us.

"The Aleuts!" he shouted. "The Aleuts!"

It was news we expected. We were prepared for it, yet there was much fear in the village of Ghalas-at. Matasaip strode from hut to hut telling everyone to be calm and not to lose time packing things that would not be needed. I took my skirt of yucca fiber, however, for I had spent many days making it and it was very pretty, and also my otter cape.

Quietly we filed out of the village along the trail that led toward the place where our canoes were hidden. The moon was growing pale and there was a faint light in the east, but a strong wind began to blow.

We had gone no farther than half a league when we were overtaken by the man who had given the warning. He spoke to Matasaip, but we all gathered around to listen to him.

"I went back to the cove after I gave the alarm," he said. "When I got there I could see the ship clearly. It is beyond the rocks that guard the harbor. It is a smaller ship than the one which belonged to the Aleuts. The sails are white instead of red."

"Could you see anyone?" Matasaip asked.

"No."

"It is not the same ship which was here last spring?"

"No."

Matasaip was silent, pondering the news. Then he told us to go on to where the canoes were and wait for him, for he was going back. It was light now and we went quickly over the dunes to the edge of the cliff and stood there while the sun rose.

The wind grew cold, but fearing that those on the ship would see the smoke we did not start a fire, though we had meal to cook for breakfast. Instead we ate a small quantity of dried abalone, and afterwards my brother Ramo climbed over the cliff. No one had been down to the rocks since the canoes were hidden so we did not know whether they were still safe or not.

While he was gone we saw a man running across the dunes. It was Nanko, carrying a message from Matasaip. He was sweating in spite of the cold and he stood trying to catch his breath. We all waited, urging him to talk, but his face was happy and we knew that he brought good news.

"Speak!" everyone said in a chorus.

"I have been running for more than a league," he said. "I cannot talk."

"You are talking," someone said.

"Speak, Nanko, speak," cried many voices.

Nanko was having fun with us. He threw out his chest and took a deep breath. He looked around at the circle of faces as if he did not understand why everyone was staring at him.

"The ship," he said at last, saying the words slowly, "does not belong to our enemies, the Aleuts.

There are white men on this ship and they have come from that place where Kimki went when he left our island."

"Has Kimki returned?" an old man broke in.

"No, but it is he who saw the white men and told them to come here."

"What do they look like?" Ulape asked.

"Are there boys on the ship?" asked Ramo, who had come back with his mouth full of something.

Everyone seemed to be talking at once.

Nanko made his face stern, which was hard for him to do because his mouth had been cut in the battle with the Aleuts and ever since it had always seemed to smile. He held up his hand for silence.

"The ship has come for one reason," he said. "To take us away from Ghalas-at."

"To what place?" I asked.

It was good news that the ship did not belong to the Aleuts. But where would the white men take us?

"I do not know to what place," he said. "Kimki knows and he has asked the white men to take us there."

Saying no more, Nanko turned back and we followed him. We were fearful of where we were going, yet we were happy, too.

Chapter 7

We took nothing with us when we thought we would have to flee, so there was much excitement as we packed our baskets. Nanko strode up and down outside the houses, urging us to hurry.

"The wind grows strong," he shouted. "The ship will leave you."

I filled two baskets with the things I wished to take. Three fine needles of whalebone, an awl for making holes, a good stone knife for scraping hides, two cooking pots, and a small box made from a shell with many earrings in it.

Ulape had two boxes of earrings, for she was vainer than I, and when she put them into her baskets, she drew a thin mark with blue clay across her nose and cheekbones. The mark meant that she was unmarried.

"The ship leaves," shouted Nanko.

"If it goes," Ulape shouted back, "it will come again after the storm."

My sister was in love with Nanko, but she laughed at him.

"Other men will come to the island," she said. "They will be far more handsome and brave than those who leave."

"You are all women of such ugliness that they will be afraid and soon go away."

The wind blew in fierce gusts as we left the village, stinging our faces with sand. Ramo hopped along far in front with one of our baskets, but before long he ran back to say that he had forgotten his fishing spear. Nanko was standing on the cliff motioning us to hurry, so I refused to let him go back for it.

The ship was anchored outside the cove and Nanko said that it could not come closer to the shore because of the high waves. They were beating against the rocks with the sound of thunder. The shore as far as I could see was rimmed with foam.

Two boats were pulled up on the beach. Beside them stood four white men and as we came down the trail, one of the men beckoned us to walk faster. He spoke to us in a language which we could not understand.

The men of our tribe, except Nanko and Chief Matasaip, were already on the ship. My brother Ramo was there too, Nanko said. He had run on ahead after I had told him that he could not go back to the village for his spear. Nanko said that he had jumped into the first boat that left the cove.

Matasaip divided the women into two groups. Then the boats were pushed into the water, and while they bobbed about we scrambled into them as best we could.

The cove was partly sheltered from the wind, but as soon as we went through the passage between the rocks and into the sea, great waves struck us. There was much confusion. Spray flew, the white men shouted at each other. The boat pitched so wildly that in one breath you could see the ship and in the next breath it had gone. Yet we came to it at last and somehow were able to climb onto the deck.

The ship was large, many times the size of our biggest canoes. It had two tall masts and between them stood a young man with blue eyes and a black beard. He was the chieftain of the white men, for he began to shout orders which they quickly obeyed. Sails rose on the tall masts and two of the men began to pull on the rope that held the anchor.

I called to my brother, knowing that he was very curious and therefore would be in the way of the men who were working. The wind drowned my voice and he did not answer. The deck was so crowded that it was hard to move, but I went from one end of it to the other, calling his name. Still there was no answer. No one had seen him.

At last I found Nanko.

I was overcome with fear. "Where is my brother?" I cried.

He repeated what he had told me on the beach, but as he spoke Ulape who stood beside him pointed toward the island. I looked out across the deck and the sea. There, running along the cliff, the fishing spear held over his head, was Ramo.

The sails had filled and the ship was now moving slowly away. Everyone was looking toward the cliff, even the white men. I ran to one of them and pointed, but he shook his head and turned from me. The ship began to move faster. Against my will, I screamed.

Chief Matasaip grasped my arm.

"We cannot wait for Ramo," he said. "If we do, the ship will be driven on the rocks."

"We must!" I shouted. "We must!"

"The ship will come back for him on another day," Matasaip said. "He will be safe. There is food for him to eat and water to drink and places to sleep."

"No," I cried.

Matasaip's face was like stone. He was not listening. I cried out once more, but my voice was lost in the howling wind. People gathered around me, saying again what Matasaip had said, yet I was not comforted by their words.

Ramo had disappeared from the cliff and I knew that he was now running along the trail that led to the beach.

The ship began to circle the kelp bed and I thought surely that it was going to return to the shore. I held my breath, waiting. Then slowly its direction changed. It pointed toward the east. At that moment I walked across the deck and, though many hands tried to hold me back, flung myself into the sea.

A wave passed over my head and I went down and down until I thought I would never behold the day again. The ship was far away when I rose. Only the sails showed through the spray. I was still clutching the basket that held all of my things, but it was very heavy and I realized that I could not swim with it in my arms. Letting it sink, I started off toward the shore.

I could barely see the two rocks that guarded the entrance to Coral Cove, but I was not fearful. Many times I had swum farther than this, although not in a storm.

I kept thinking over and over as I swam how I would punish Ramo when I reached the shore, yet when I felt the sand under my feet and saw him standing at the edge of the waves, holding his fishing spear and looking so forlorn, I forgot all those things I planned to do. Instead I fell to my knees and put my arms around him.

The ship had disappeared.

"When will it come back?" Ramo asked. There were tears in his eyes.

"Soon," I said.

The only thing that made me angry was that my beautiful skirt of yucca fibers, which I had worked on so long and carefully, was ruined.

Chapter 8

The wind blew strong as we climbed the trail, covering the mesa with sand that sifted around our legs and shut out the sky. Since it was not possible to find our way back, we took shelter among some rocks. We stayed there until night fell. Then the wind lessened and the moon came out and by its light we reached the village.

The huts looked like ghosts in the cold light. As we neared them I heard a strange sound like that of running feet. I thought that it was a sound made by the wind, but when we came closer I saw dozens of wild dogs scurrying around through the huts. They ran from us, snarling as they went.

The pack must have slunk into the village soon after we left, for it had gorged itself upon the abalone we had not taken. It had gone everywhere searching for food, and Ramo and I had to look hard to find enough for our supper. While we ate beside a small fire I could hear the dogs on the hill not far away, and through the night their howls came to me on the wind. But when the sun rose and I went out of the hut, the pack trotted off toward its lair which was at the north side of the island, in a large cave.

That day we spent gathering food. The wind blew and the waves crashed against the shore so that we could not go out on the rocks. I gathered gull eggs on the cliff and Ramo speared a string of small fish in one of the tide pools. He brought them home, walking proudly with the string over his back. He felt that in this way he had made up for the trouble he had caused.

With the seeds I had gathered in a ravine, we had a plentiful meal, although I had to cook it on a flat rock. My bowls were at the bottom of the sea.

The wild dogs came again that night. Drawn by the scent of fish, they sat on the hill, barking and growling at each other. I could see the light from the fire shining in their eyes. At dawn they left.

The ocean was calm on this day and we were able to hunt abalone among the rocks. From seaweed we wove a rough basket which we filled before the sun was overhead. On the way home, carrying the abalone between us, Ramo and I stopped on the cliff. The air was clear and we could look far out to sea in the direction the ship had gone.

"Will it come back today?" Ramo asked.

"It may," I answered him, though I did not think so. "More likely it will come after many suns, for the country where it has gone is far off."

Ramo looked up at me. His black eyes shone.

"I do not care if the ship never comes," he said.

"Why do you say this?" I asked him.

Ramo thought, making a hole in the earth with the point of his spear.

"Why?" I asked again.

"Because I like it here with you," he said. "It is more fun than when the others were here. Tomorrow I am going to where the canoes are hidden and bring one back to Coral Cove. We will use it to fish in and to go looking around the island."

"They are too heavy for you to put into the water."

"You will see."

Ramo threw out his chest. Around his neck was a string of sea-elephant teeth which someone had left behind. It was much too large for him and the teeth were broken, but they rattled as he thrust the spear down between us.

"You forget that I am the son of Chowig," he said.

"I do not forget," I answered. "But you are a small son. Someday you will be tall and strong and then you will be able to handle a big canoe."

"I am the son of Chowig," he said again, and as he spoke his eyes suddenly grew large. "I am his son and since he is dead I have taken his place. I am now Chief of Ghalas-at. All my wishes must be obeyed."

"But first you must become a man. As is the custom, therefore, I will have to whip you with a switch of nettles and then tie you to a red-ant hill."

Ramo grew pale. He had seen the rites of manhood given in our tribe and remembered them. Quickly I said, "Since there are no men to give the rites, perhaps you will not have to undergo the nettles and the ants, Chief Ramo."

"I do not know if this name suits me," he said, smiling. He tossed his spear at a passing gull. "I will think of something better."

I watched him stride off to get the spear, a little boy with thin arms and legs like sticks, wearing a big string of sea-elephant teeth. Now that he had become Chief of Ghalas-at, I would have even more trouble with him, but I wanted to run after him and take him in my arms.

"I have thought of a name," he said when he came back.

"What is it?" I asked solemnly.

"I am Chief Tanyositlopai."

"That is a very long name and hard to say."

"You will soon learn," Chief Tanyositlopai said.

I had no thought of letting Chief Tanyositlopai go

alone to the place where the canoes were hidden, but the next morning when I awoke I found that Ramo was not in the hut. He was not outside either, and I knew then that he had gotten up in the dark and left by himself.

I was frightened. I thought of all that might befall him. He had climbed down the kelp rope once before, but he would have trouble pushing even the smallest of the canoes off the rocks. And if he did get one afloat without hurting himself, would he be able to paddle around the sandspit where the tides ran fast?

Thinking of these dangers, I started off to overtake him.

I had not gone far along the trail before I began to wonder if I should not let him go to the cliff by himself. There was no way of telling when the ship would come back for us. Until it did, we were alone upon the island. Ramo therefore would have to become a man sooner than if we were not alone, since I would need his help in many ways.

Suddenly I turned around and took the trail toward Coral Cove. If Ramo could put the canoe in the water and get through the tides that raced around the sandspit, he would reach the harbor when the sun was tall in the sky. I would be waiting on the beach, for what was the fun of a voyage if no one were there to greet him?

I put Ramo out of my mind as I searched the rocks for mussels. I thought of the food we would need to gather and how best to protect it from the wild dogs when we were not in the village. I thought also of the ship. I tried to remember what Matasaip had said to me. For the first time I began to wonder if the ship would ever return. I wondered about this as I pried the shells off the rocks, and I would stop and look fearfully at the empty sea that stretched away farther than my eyes could reach.

The sun moved higher. There was no sign of Ramo. I began to feel uneasy. The basket was filled and I carried it up to the mesa.

From here I looked down on the harbor and farther on along the coast to the spit that thrust out like a fishhook into the ocean. I could see the small waves sliding up the sand and beyond them a curving line of foam where the currents raced.

I waited on the mesa until the sun was overhead. Then I hurried back to the village, hoping that Ramo might have come back while I was gone. The hut was empty.

Quickly I dug a hole for the shellfish, rolled a heavy stone over the opening to protect them from the wild dogs, and started off toward the south part of the island.

Two trails led there, one on each side of a long sand dune. Ramo was not on the trail I was traveling and, thinking that he might be coming back out of sight along the other one, I called to him as I ran. I heard no answer. But did hear, far off, the barking of dogs.

The barking grew louder as I came closer to the cliff. It would die away and after a short silence start up again. The sound came from the opposite side of the dunes, and leaving the trail I climbed upward through the sand to its top.

A short distance beyond the dune, near the cliff, I saw the pack of wild dogs. There were many of them and they were moving around in a circle.

In the middle of the circle was Ramo. He was lying on his back, and had a deep wound in his throat. He lay very still.

When I picked him up I knew that he was dead. There were other wounds on his body from the teeth of the wild dogs. He had been dead a long time and from his footsteps on the earth I could see that he had never reached the cliff.

Two dogs lay on the ground not far from him, and in the side of one of them was his broken spear.

I carried Ramo back to the village, reaching it when the sun was far down. The dogs followed me all the way, but when I had laid him down in the hut, and came out with a club in my hand, they trotted off to a low hill. A big gray dog with long curling hair and yellow eyes was their leader and he went last.

It was growing dark, but I followed them up the hill. Slowly they retreated in front of me, not making a sound. I followed them across two hills and a small valley to a third hill whose face was a ledge of rock. At one end of the ledge was a cave. One by one the dogs went into it.

The mouth of the cave was too wide and high to fill with rocks. I gathered brush and made a fire, thinking that I would push it back into the cave. Through the night I would feed it and push it farther and farther back. But there was not enough brush for this.

When the moon rose I left the cave and went off through the valley and over the three hills to my home.

All night I sat there with the body of my brother and did not sleep. I vowed that some day I would go back and kill the wild dogs in the cave. I would kill all of them. I thought of how I would do it, but mostly I thought of Ramo, my brother.

Chapter 9

I do not remember much of this time, except that many suns rose and set. I thought about what I was going to do now that I was alone. I did not leave the village. Not until I had eaten all of the abalones did I leave and then only to gather more.

Yet I do remember the day that I decided I would never live in the village again.

It was a morning of thick fog and the sound of far-off waves breaking on the shore. I had never noticed before how silent the village was. Fog crept in and out of the empty huts. It made shapes as it drifted and they reminded me of all the people who were dead and those who were gone. The noise of the surf seemed to be their voices speaking.

I sat for a long time, seeing these shapes and hearing the voices, until the sun came out and the fog vanished. Then I made a fire against the wall of the house. When it was burned to the earth I started a fire in another house. Thus, one by one, I destroyed them all so that there were only ashes left to mark the village of Ghalas-at.

There was nothing to take away with me except a basket of food. I therefore traveled fast and before night fell I reached the place where I had decided to live until the ship returned.

This place lay on a headland a half league to the west of Coral Cove. There was a large rock on that headland and two stunted trees. Behind the rock was a clear place about ten steps across, which was sheltered from the wind, from which I could see the harbor and the ocean. A spring of water flowed from a ravine nearby.

That night I climbed onto the rock to sleep. It was flat on top and wide enough for me to stretch out. Also it was so high from the ground that I did not need to fear the wild dogs while I was sleeping. I had not seen them again since the day they had killed Ramo, but I was sure they would soon come to my new camp.

The rock was also a safe place to store the food I had brought with me and everything I should gather. Since it was still winter and any day the ship might return, there was no use to store food I would not need. This gave me time to make weapons to protect myself from the dogs, which I felt would sometime attack me, to kill them all, one by one.

I had a club I found in one of the huts, but I needed a bow and arrows and a large spear. The spear which I had taken from the slain dog was too small. It was good for spearing fish and little else.

The laws of Ghalas-at forbade the making of weapons by women of the tribe, so I went out to search for any that might have been left behind. I went first to where the village had been and sifted the ashes for spearheads, and then, finding none, to the place where the canoes were hidden, believing that weapons might have been stored there with the food and water.

I found nothing in the canoes under the cliff. Then, remembering the chest the Aleuts had brought to shore, I set out for Coral Cove. I had seen that chest on the beach during the battle but did not remember that the hunters had taken it with them when they fled.

The beach was empty except for rows of seaweed

washed in by the storm. The tide was out and I looked in the place where the chest had lain.

It was just below the ledge Ulape and I had stood on while we watched the battle. The sand was smooth and I dug many small holes with a stick. I dug in a wide circle, thinking that the storm might have covered it with sand.

Near the center of the circle the stick hit something hard, which I was sure was a rock, but as I dug deeper with my hands I saw it was the black lid of the chest.

All morning I worked, moving the sand away. The chest lay deep from the washing of the waves and I did not try to dig it out, but only so I could raise the lid.

As the sun rose high the tide came rushing up the beach and filled the hole with sand. Each wave covered the chest deeper until it was completely hidden. I stood on the place, bracing myself against the waves, so that I would not have to look for it again. When the tide turned I began to dig with my feet, working them down and down, and then with my hands.

The chest was filled with beads and bracelets and earrings of many colors. I forgot about the spearheads I had come for. I held each of the trinkets to the sun, turning them so that they caught the light. I put on the longest string of beads, which were blue, and a pair of blue bracelets, which exactly fitted my wrists, and walked down the shore, admiring myself.

I walked the whole length of the cove. The beads and the bracelets made tinkling sounds. I felt like the bride of a chief as I walked there by the waves.

I came to the foot of the trail where the battle had been fought. Suddenly I remembered those who had died there and the men who had brought the jewels I was wearing. I went back to the chest. For a long time I stood beside it, looking at the bracelets and the beads hanging from my neck, so beautiful and bright in the sun. "They do not belong to the Aleuts," I said, "they belong to me." But even as I said this I knew that I never could wear them.

One by one I took them off. I also took the rest of the beads from the chest. Then I walked through the waves and flung them all far away, out into the deep water.

There were no iron spearheads in the chest. I closed the lid and covered it with sand.

I looked along the bottom of the trail, but finding nothing there that I could use, gave up my search.

For many days I did not think of the weapons again, not until the wild dogs came one night and sat under the rock and howled. They were gone at daylight, but not far. During the day I could see them slinking through the brush, watching me.

That night they came back to the headland. I had buried what was left of my supper, but they dug it up, snarling and fighting among themselves over the scraps. Then they began to pace back and forth at the foot of the rock, sniffing the air, for they could smell my tracks and knew that I was somewhere near.

For a long time I lay on the rock while they trotted around below me. The rock was high and they could not climb it, but I was still fearful. As I lay there I wondered what would happen to me if I went against the law of our tribe which forbade the making of weapons by women—if I did not think of it at all and made those things which I must have to protect myself.

Would the four winds blow in from the four

directions of the world and smother me as I made the weapons? Or would the earth tremble, as many said, and bury me beneath its falling rocks? Or, as others said, would the sea rise over the island in a terrible flood? Would the weapons break in my hands at the moment when my life was in danger, which is what my father had said?

I thought about these things for two days and on the third night when the wild dogs returned to the rock, I made up my mind that no matter what befell me I would make the weapons. In the morning I set about it, though I felt very fearful.

I wished to use a sea elephant's tusk for the tip of the spear because it is hard and of the right shape. There were many of these animals on the shore near my camp, but I lacked a weapon with which to kill one. Our men usually hunted them with a strong net made of bull kelp, which they threw over an animal while it slept. To do this at least three men were needed, and even then the sea elephant often dragged the net into the sea and got away.

I used instead the root of a tree which I shaped into a point and hardened in the fire. This I bound to a long shaft, with the green sinews of a seal I killed with a rock.

The bow and arrows took more time and caused me great difficulty. I had a bowstring, but wood which could be bent and yet had the proper strength was not easy to find. I searched the ravines for several days before I found it, trees being very scarce on the Island of the Blue Dolphins. Wood for the arrows was easier to find, and also the stone for the tips and the feathers for the ends of the shafts.

Gathering these things was not the most of the trouble. I had seen the weapons made, but I knew little about it. I had seen my father sitting in the hut on winter nights scraping the wood for the shafts, chipping the stones for the tips, and tying the feathers, yet I had watched him and really seen nothing. I had watched, but not with the eye of one who would ever do it.

For this reason I took many days and had many failures before I fashioned a bow and arrows that could be used.

Wherever I went now, whether to the shore when I gathered shellfish or to the ravine for water, I carried this weapon in a sling on my back. I practiced with it and also with the spear.

The dogs did not come to the camp during the time I was making the weapons, though every night I could hear them howling.

Once, after the weapons were made, I saw the leader of the pack, the one with the gray hair and the yellow eyes watching me from the brush. I had gone to the ravine for water and he stood on the hill above the spring, looking down at me. He stood very quiet, with only his head showing over the top of a cholla bush. He was too far away for me to reach him with an arrow.

Wherever I went during the day, I felt secure with my new weapons, and I waited patiently for the time when I could use them against the wild dogs that had killed Ramo. I did not go to the cave where they had their lair since I was sure that they would soon come to the camp. Yet every night I climbed onto the rock to sleep.

After the first night I spent there, which was uncomfortable because of the uneven places in the rock, I carried dry seaweed up from the beach and made a bed for myself.

It was a pleasant place to stay, there on the headland. The stars were bright overhead and I lay and counted the ones that I knew and gave names to many that I did not know.

In the morning the gulls flew out from their nests in the crevices of the cliff. They circled down to the tide pools where they stood first on one leg and then the other, splashing water over themselves and combing their feathers with curved beaks. Then they flew off down the shore to look for food. Beyond the kelp beds pelicans were already hunting, soaring high over the clear water, diving straight down, if they sighted a fish, to strike the sea with a great splash that I could hear.

I also watched the otter hunting in the kelp. These shy little animals had come back soon after the Aleuts had left and now there seemed to be as many of them as before. The early morning sun shone like gold on their glossy pelts.

Yet as I lay there on the high rock, looking at the stars, I thought about the ship which belonged to the white men. And at dawn, as light spread across the sea, my first glance was toward the little harbor of Coral Cove. Every morning I would look for the ship there, thinking that it might have come in the night. And each morning I would see nothing except the birds flying over the sea.

When there were people in Ghalas-at I was always up before the sun and busy with many things. But now that there was little to do I did not leave the rock until the sun was high. I would eat and then go to the spring and take a bath in the warm water. Afterwards I went down to the shore where I could gather a few abalones and sometimes spear a fish for my supper. Before darkness fell I climbed onto the rock and watched the sea until it slowly disappeared in the night.

The ship did not come and thus winter passed and the spring.

Chapter 10

Summer is the best time on the Island of the Blue Dolphins. The sun is warm then and the winds blow milder out of the west, sometimes out of the south.

It was during these days that the ship might return and now I spent most of my time on the rock, looking out from the high headland into the east, toward the country where my people had gone, across the sea that was never-ending.

Once while I watched I saw a small object which I took to be the ship, but a stream of water rose from it and I knew that it was a whale spouting. During those summer days I saw nothing else.

The first storm of winter ended my hopes. If the white men's ship were coming for me it would have come during the time of good weather. Now I would have to wait until winter was gone, maybe longer.

The thought of being alone on the island while so many suns rose from the sea and went slowly back into the sea filled my heart with loneliness. I had not felt so lonely before because I was sure that the ship would return as Matasaip had said it would. Now my hopes were dead. Now I was really alone. I could not eat much, nor could I sleep without dreaming terrible dreams.

The storm blew out of the north, sending big waves against the island and winds so strong that I was unable to stay on the rock. I moved my bed to the foot of the rock and for protection kept a fire going throughout the night. I slept there five times.

The first night the dogs came and stood outside the ring made by the fire. I killed three of them with arrows, but not the leader, and they did not come again.

On the sixth day, when the storm had ended, I went to the place where the canoes had been hidden, and let myself down over the cliff. This part of the shore was sheltered from the wind and I found the canoes just as they had been left. The dried food was still good, but the water was stale, so I went back to the spring and filled a fresh basket.

I had decided during the days of the storm, when I had given up hope of seeing the ship, that I would take one of the canoes and go to the country that lay toward the east. I remembered how Kimki, before he had gone, had asked the advice of his ancestors who had lived many ages in the past, who had come to the island from that country, and likewise the advice of Zuma, the medicine man who held power over the wind and the seas. But these things I could not do, for Zuma had been killed by the Aleuts, and in all my life I had never been able to speak with the dead, though many times I had tried.

Yet I cannot say that I was really afraid as I stood there on the shore. I knew that my ancestors had crossed the sea in their canoes, coming from that place which lay beyond. Kimki too had crossed the sea. I was not nearly so skilled with a canoe as these men, but I must say that whatever might befall me on the endless waters did not trouble me. It meant far less than the thought of staying on the island alone, without a home or companions, pursued by wild dogs, where everything reminded me of those who were dead and those who had gone away.

Of the four canoes stored there against the cliff, I

chose the smallest, which was still very heavy because it could carry six people. The task that faced me was to push it down the rocky shore and into the water, a distance four or five times its length.

This I did by first removing all the large rocks in front of the canoe. I then filled in all these holes with pebbles and along this path laid down long strips of kelp, making a slippery bed. The shore was steep and once I got the canoe to move with its own weight, it slid down the path and into the water.

The sun was in the west when I left the shore. The sea was calm behind the high cliffs. Using the two-bladed paddle I quickly skirted the south part of the island. As I reached the sandspit the wind struck. I was paddling from the back of the canoe because you can go faster kneeling there, but I could not handle it in the wind.

Kneeling in the middle of the canoe, I paddled hard and did not pause until I had gone through the tides that run fast around the sandspit. There were many small waves and I was soon wet, but as I came out from behind the spit the spray lessened and the waves grew long and rolling. Though it would have been easier to go the way they slanted, this would have taken me in the wrong direction. I therefore kept them on my left hand, as well as the island, which grew smaller and smaller, behind me.

At dusk I looked back. The Island of the Blue Dolphins had disappeared. This was the first time that I felt afraid.

There were only hills and valleys of water around me now. When I was in a valley I could see nothing and when the canoe rose out of it, only the ocean stretching away and away.

Night fell and I drank from the basket. The water cooled my throat.

The sea was black and there was no difference between it and the sky. The waves made no sound among themselves, only faint noises as they went under the canoe or struck against it. Sometimes the noises seemed angry and at other times like people laughing. I was not hungry because of my fear.

The first star made me feel less afraid. It came out low in the sky and it was in front of me, toward the east. Other stars began to appear all around, but it was this one I kept my gaze upon. It was in the figure that we call a serpent, a star which shone green and which I knew. Now and then it was hidden by mist, yet it always came out brightly again.

Without this star I would have been lost, for the waves never changed. They came always from the same direction and in a manner that kept pushing me away from the place I wanted to reach. For this reason the canoe made a path in the black water like a snake. But somehow I kept moving toward the star which shone in the east.

This star rose high and then I kept the North Star on my left hand, the one we call "the star that does not move." The wind grew quiet. Since it always died down when the night was half over, I knew how long I had been traveling and how far away the dawn was.

About this time I found that the canoe was leaking. Before dark I had emptied one of the baskets in which food was stored and used it to dip out the water that came over the sides. The water that now moved around my knees was not from the waves.

I stopped paddling and worked with the basket until the bottom of the canoe was almost dry. Then I searched around, feeling in the dark along the smooth planks, and found the place near the bow where the water was seeping through a crack as long as my hand and the width of a finger. Most of the time it was out of the sea, but it leaked whenever the canoe dipped forward in the waves.

The places between the planks were filled with black pitch which we gather along the shore. Lacking this, I tore a piece of fiber from my skirt and pressed it into the crack, which held back the water.

Dawn broke in a clear sky and as the sun came out of the waves I saw that it was far off on my left. During the night I had drifted south of the place I wished to go, so I changed my direction and paddled along the path made by the rising sun.

There was no wind on this morning and the long waves went quietly under the canoe. I therefore moved faster than during the night.

I was very tired, but more hopeful than I had been since I left the island. If the good weather did not change I would cover many leagues before dark. Another night and another day might bring me within sight of the shore toward which I was going.

Not long after dawn, while I was thinking of this strange place and what it would look like, the canoe began to leak again. This crack was between the same planks but was a larger one and close to where I was kneeling.

The fiber I tore from my skirt and pushed into the crack held back most of the water which seeped in whenever the canoe rose and fell with the waves. Yet I could see that the planks were weak from one end to the other, probably from the canoe being stored so long in the sun, and that they might open along their whole length if the waves grew rougher.

It was suddenly clear to me that it was dangerous to go on. The voyage would take two more days, perhaps longer. By turning back to the island I would not have nearly so far to travel.

Still I could not make up my mind to do so. The sea was calm and I had come far. The thought of turning back after all this labor was more than I could bear. Even greater was the thought of the deserted island I would return to, of living there alone and forgotten. For how many suns and how many moons?

The canoe drifted idly on the calm sea while these thoughts went over and over in my mind, but when I saw the water seeping through the crack again, I picked up the paddle. There was no choice except to turn back toward the island.

I knew that only by the best of fortune would I ever reach it.

The wind did not blow until the sun was overhead. Before that time I covered a good distance, pausing only when it was necessary to dip water from the canoe. With the wind I went more slowly and had to stop more often because of the water spilling over the sides, but the leak did not grow worse.

This was my first good fortune. The next was when a swarm of dolphins appeared. They came swimming out of the west, but as they saw the canoe they turned around in a great circle and began to follow me. They swam up slowly and so close that I could see their eyes, which are large and the color of the ocean. Then they swam on ahead of the canoe, crossing back and forth in front of it, diving in and out, as if they were weaving a piece of cloth with their broad snouts.

Dolphins are animals of good omen. It made me happy to have them swimming around the canoe, and though my hands had begun to bleed from the chafing of the paddle, just watching them made me forget the pain. I was very lonely before they appeared, but now I felt that I had friends with me and did not feel the same.

The blue dolphins left me shortly before dusk. They left as quickly as they had come, going on into the west, but for a long time I could see the last of the sun shining on them. After night fell I could still see them in my thoughts and it was because of this that I kept on paddling when I wanted to lie down and sleep.

More than anything, it was the blue dolphins that took me back home.

Fog came with the night, yet from time to time I could see the star that stands high in the west, the red star called Magat which is part of the figure that looks like a crawfish and is known by that name. The crack in the planks grew wider so I had to stop often to fill it with fiber and to dip out the water.

The night was very long, longer than the night before. Twice I dozed kneeling there in the canoe, though I was more afraid than I had ever been. But the morning broke clear and in front of me lay the dim line of the island like a great fish sunning itself on the sea.

I reached it before the sun was high, the sandspit and its tides that bore me into the shore. My legs were stiff from kneeling and as the canoe struck the sand I fell when I rose to climb out. I crawled through the shallow water and up the beach. There I lay for a long time, hugging the sand in happiness.

I was too tired to think of the wild dogs. Soon I fell asleep.

Chapter 11

I was awakened by the waves dragging at my feet. Night had come, but being too tired to leave the sandspit, I crawled to a higher place where I would be safe from the tide, and again went to sleep.

In the morning I found the canoe a short distance away. I took the baskets, my spear, and the bow and arrows, and turned the canoe over so that the tides could not take it out to sea. I then climbed to the headland where I had lived before.

I felt as if I had been gone a long time as I stood there looking down from the high rock. I was happy to be home. Everything that I saw—the otter playing in the kelp, the rings of foam around the rocks that guarded the harbor, the gulls flying, the tides moving past the sandspit—filled me with happiness.

I was surprised that I felt this way, for it was only a short time ago that I had stood on this same rock and felt that I could not bear to live here another day.

I looked out at the blue water stretching away and all the fear I had felt during the time of the voyage came back to me. On the morning I first sighted the island and it had seemed like a great fish sunning itself, I thought that someday I would make the canoe over and go out once more to look for the country that lay beyond the ocean. Now I knew that I would never go again.

The Island of the Blue Dolphins was my home; I had no other. It would be my home until the white men returned in their ship. But even if they came soon, before next summer, I could not live without a roof or a place to store my food. I would have to build a house. But where?

That night I slept on the rock and the next day I began the search. The morning was clear, but to the north banks of clouds hung low. Before long they would move in across the island and behind them many other storms were waiting. I had no time to waste.

I needed a place that was sheltered from the wind, not too far from Coral Cove, and close to a good spring. There were two such places on the island— one on the headland and the other less than a league to the west. The headland seemed to be the more favorable of the two, but since I had not been to the other for a long time I decided to go there and make certain.

The first thing I found, which I had forgotten, was that this place was near the wild dogs' lair. As soon as I drew near to it the leader came to the opening of the cave and watched me with his yellow eyes. If I built a hut here I would have to kill him and his pack. I planned to do this anyway, but it would take much time.

The spring was better than the one near the headland, being less brackish and having a steadier flow of water. Besides it was much easier to reach, since it came from the side of a hill and not from a ravine as the other one did. It was also close to the cliff and a ridge of rocks which would shelter my house.

The rocks were not so high as those on the headland and therefore would give me less protection from the wind, yet they were high enough, and from them I could see the north coast and Coral Cove.

The thing that made me decide on the place to build my house was the sea elephants.

The cliffs here fell away easily to a wide shelf that was partly covered when the tide came in. It was a good place for sea elephants because they could crawl halfway up the cliff if the day were stormy. On fair days they could fish among the pools or lie on the rocks.

The bull is very large and often weighs as much as thirty men. The cows are much smaller, but they make more noise than the bulls, screaming and barking through the whole day and sometimes at night. The babies are noisy, too.

On this morning the tide was low and most of the animals were far out, just hundreds of specks against the waves, yet the noise they made was deafening. I stayed there the rest of the day, looking around, and that night. At dawn when the clamor started again I left and went back to the headland.

There was another place to the south where I could have built my house, near the destroyed village of Ghalas-at, but I did not want to go there because it would remind me of the people who were gone. Also the wind blew strong in this place, blowing against the dunes which cover the middle part of the island so that most of the time sand is moving everywhere.

Rain fell that night and lasted for two days. I made a shelter of brush at the foot of the rock, which kept off some of the water, and ate the food I had stored in the basket. I could not build a fire because of the rain and I was very cold.

On the third day the rain ceased and I went out to look for things which I would need in building the house. I likewise needed poles for a fence. I would soon kill the wild dogs, but there were many small red foxes on the island. They were so numerous that I could never hope to get rid of them either by traps or with arrows. They were clever thieves and nothing I stored would be safe until I had built a fence.

The morning was fresh from the rain. The smell of the tide pools was strong. Sweet odors came from the wild grasses in the ravines and from the sand plants on the dunes. I sang as I went down the trail to the beach and along the beach to the sandspit. I felt that the day was an omen of good fortune.

It was a good day to begin my new home.

Chapter 12

Many years before, two whales had washed up on the sandspit. Most of the bones had been taken away to make ornaments, but ribs were still there, half-buried in the sand.

These I used in making the fence. One by one I dug them up and carried them to the headland. They were long and curved, and when I had scooped out holes and set them in the earth they stood taller than I did.

I put the ribs together with their edges almost touching, and standing so that they curved outward, which made them impossible to climb. Between them I wove many strands of bull kelp, which shrinks as it dries and pulls very tight. I would have used seal sinew to bind the ribs together, for this is stronger than kelp, but wild animals like it and soon would have gnawed the fence down. Much time went into its building. It would have taken me longer except that the rock made one end of the fence and part of a side.

For a place to go in and out, I dug a hole under the fence just wide and deep enough to crawl through. The bottom and sides I lined with stones. On the outside I covered the hole with a mat woven of brush to shed the rain, and on the inside with a flat rock which I was strong enough to move.

I was able to take eight steps between the sides of the fence, which gave me all the room I would need to store the things I gathered and wished to protect.

I built the fence first because it was too cold to

sleep on the rock and I did not like to sleep in the shelter I had made until I was safe from the wild dogs.

The house took longer to build than the fence because it rained many days and because the wood I needed was scarce.

There was a legend among our people that the island had once been covered with tall trees. This was a long time ago, at the beginning of the world when Tumaiyowit and Mukat ruled. The two gods quarreled about many things. Tumaiyowit wished people to die. Mukat did not. Tumaiyowit angrily went down, down to another world under this world, taking his belongings with him, so people die because he did.

In that time there were tall trees, but now there were only a few in the ravines and these were small and crooked. It was very hard to find one that would make a good pole. I searched many days, going out early in the morning and coming back at night, before I found enough for a house.

I used the rock for the back of the house and the front I left open since the wind did not blow from this direction. The poles I made of equal length, using fire to cut them as well as a stone knife which caused me much difficulty because I had never made such a tool before. There were four poles on each side, set in the earth, and twice that many for the roof. These I bound together with sinew and covered with female kelp, which has broad leaves.

The winter was half over before I finished the house, but I slept there every night and felt secure because of the strong fence. The foxes came when I was cooking my food and stood outside gazing through the cracks, and the wild dogs also came, gnawing at the whale ribs, growling because they could not get in.

I shot two of them, but not the leader.

While I was building the fence and the house, I ate shellfish and perch which I cooked on a flat rock. Afterwards I made two utensils. Along the shore there were stones that the sea had worn smooth. Most of them were round, but I found two with hollow places in the center which I deepened and broadened by rubbing them with sand. Using these to cook in, I saved the juices of the fish which are good and were wasted before.

For cooking seeds and roots I wove a tight basket of fine reeds, which was easy because I had learned how to do it from my sister Ulape. After the basket had dried in the sun, I gathered lumps of pitch on the shore, softened them over the fire, and rubbed them on the inside of the basket so that it would hold water. By heating small stones and dropping them into a mixture of water and seeds in the basket I could make gruel.

I made a place for fire in the floor of my house, hollowing it out and lining it with rocks. In the village of Ghalas-at we made new fires every night, but now I made one fire which I covered with ashes when I went to bed. The next night I would remove the ashes and blow on the embers. In this way I saved myself much work.

There were many gray mice on the island and now that I had food to keep from one meal to the other, I needed a safe place to put it. On the face of the rock, which was the back wall of my house, were several cracks as high as my shoulder. These I cut out and smoothed to make shelves where I could store my food and the mice could not reach it.

By the time winter was over and grass began to show green on the hills my house was comfortable. I was sheltered from the wind and rain and prowling animals. I could cook anything I wished to eat. Everything I wanted was there at hand.

It was now time to make plans for getting rid of the wild dogs which had killed my brother and would kill me should they ever come upon me unarmed. I needed another and heavier spear, also a larger bow and sharper arrows. To collect the material for these weapons, I searched the whole island, taking many suns to do it. This left only the nights to work on them. Since I could not see well by the dim fire I used for cooking, I made lamps of the dried bodies of little fish we call *sai-sai*.

The *sai-sai* is the color of silver and not much bigger than a finger. On nights when the moon shines full, these little fish come swimming out of the sea in schools so thick that you can almost walk on them. They come with the waves and twist and turn on the sand as if they were dancing.

I caught many basketfuls of *sai-sai* and put them out in the sun. Hung up by their tails from the poles of the roof, they made much odor, but burned with a very clear light.

I made the bow and arrows first and was pleased when I tried them that I could shoot farther and much straighter than I had before.

The spear I left to the last. I wondered, as I smoothed and shaped the long handle and fitted a stone collar around the end both to give the spear weight and to hold the spear point, if I could make this point the way the men of our tribe did, from the tooth of a sea elephant.

Many nights I thought about it, wondering how I

could possibly kill one of these great beasts. I could not use a net of kelp, because that needed the strength of several men. Nor could I remember that a bull elephant had ever been killed with an arrow or with a spear. Only after they had been caught in a net were they killed and then with a club. We killed many cows for their oil, using spears, but the teeth were not large.

How I would do this, I did not know. Yet the more I thought about it, the greater was my determination to try, for there was nothing to be found on the island that made such good spear points as the tusklike teeth of the bull sea elephant.

Chapter 13

I did not sleep much the night before I went to the place of the sea elephants. I thought again about the law that forbade women to make weapons. I wondered if my arrows would go straight and, if they did, would they pierce the animal's tough hide. What if one of the bulls turned on me? What if I were injured and then had to fight the wild dogs as I dragged myself homeward?

I thought about these things most of the night, but with the sun I was up and on my way to the place where the sea elephants lived.

When I reached the cliff, the animals had left the reef and gathered along the shore. Like gray boulders the bulls sat on the pebbly slope. Below them the cows and their babies played in the waves.

Perhaps it is not right to speak of young sea elephants as babies, for they are as large as a man. But they are still babies in many ways. They follow their mothers around, waddling along on their flippers like children learning to walk, making crying sounds and sounds of pleasure that only the young make. And before they will leave the shore and learn to swim their mothers have to push them into the sea, which is often difficult to do because of their size.

Some distance separated the bulls from each other, for they are bad-tempered, very jealous by nature and quick to fight over anything that displeases them. There were six of them below me on the slope, each sitting alone like a great chief, watching his herd of cows and babies.

The cow has a smooth body and a face that looks much like that of a mouse, with a sharp-pointed nose and whiskers, but the bull is different. His nose has a large hump on it which hangs down over his mouth. His skin is rough and looks like wet earth that has dried in the sun and cracked. He is an ugly animal.

From the top of the cliff I looked down at each of the sea elephants and tried to choose the smallest of the six.

They were all the same size save one, which was the farthest from me and partly hidden by a rock. He was about half as large as the others, a young bull. Since no cows were playing among the waves in front of him, I knew that he did not have a herd of his own, and for that reason would not be so wary or quickly angered.

Quietly I let myself down over the edge of the cliff. To reach him I had to pass behind the others, being careful not to alarm them. They fear nothing and would not move if they saw me, but it was better, I thought, not to put them on their guard. I carried my new bow, which was almost as tall as I was, and five arrows.

The path was rough and covered with small stones. I took pains not to send them tumbling down the slope. I was also careful not to be seen by the cows, which get alarmed easily and would have warned the rest of the herd with their cries.

I crawled behind a big rock near the young bull. I then got to my feet and fitted an arrow to the bow, although I suddenly remembered my father's warning that, because I was a woman, the bow would break.

The sun was far in the west, but luckily my shadow fell away from the young bull. The distance between us was short and his back was turned squarely toward me. Still I did not know where to place the first arrow, whether in his shoulders or in his head. The skin of the sea elephant is rough, yet very thin, but beneath it are thick layers of fat, and though his body is large, his head is small and makes a poor target.

While I stood there behind the rock, not knowing what to do, again aware of my father's warning that a bow in the hands of a woman would always break in a time of danger, the animal began to move toward the shore. At first I thought that by some chance he had heard me. I soon saw that he was on his way toward the cows that belonged to the old bull sitting nearby.

The sea elephant moves fast in spite of his size, waddling along on his great flippers which he uses like hands. The bull was nearing the water. I let the arrow go and it went straight. At the last instant he changed direction and, though the bow did not break, the arrow passed harmlessly to one side.

I had failed to notice that the old bull was moving down the slope until I heard stones grating against each other. Quickly he overtook his rival and with a single thrust of his shoulders overturned him. The young bull stood as high as a tall man and was twice that length, yet from the force of the blow he rolled into the water and lay there stunned.

The old bull bore down upon him, swinging his head and bellowing so loud it echoed against the cliffs. The herd of cows and calves, who were lying in the waves and scratching their backs with their flippers, stopped to watch the battle.

Two of the cows were in the bull's path as he waddled toward his rival, but he went over them as if they were small stones. Using his tusklike teeth, he ripped a long gash in the young bull's side.

The young bull raised himself and as he turned his small eyes shone fiercely red. When the old bull slashed at him again, he struck first and sunk his teeth into the other's neck. He did not let go and the two rolled over in the waves, splashing water high into the air.

The cows had scattered by now, but the other bulls still sat quietly on the slope.

The two fighters paused, getting ready for a new attack. It was a good chance to send an arrow into the young bull, who lay on his back with his teeth still grasping the other's neck. But I hoped that he would win the battle, and I stood there and did not move.

The old bull had many deep scars on his head and shoulders from battles he had fought before. Suddenly he lashed out with his tail, trying to loose the hold on his neck, and struck the side of a rock. With his tail against the rock, he flung his body out of the water and thus broke away.

He came quickly up the slope, his great mouth open, the young bull close behind him. He came toward me and, in haste to get out of his way, not knowing whether he was bent on attacking me, I stepped back. In doing so, I tripped over a stone and fell to my knees.

I felt a sharp pain in my leg, but was quickly up. By this time the old bull had whirled around and turned upon his pursuer so fast that the young bull was taken by surprise. Again the young bull's flank was ripped deep, and again the force of the blow threw him backward into the water.

The waves grew redder from his blood, but this time he rolled over and was waiting for the charge. He met the old bull with his shoulder. The sound was like rocks crashing together. Once more the young bull caught the other's throat, and together they disappeared beneath a wave. When they came up they were still locked together.

The sun had gone down and it was so dark I could no longer see clearly. My leg had now begun to hurt. Since I had a long way to go, I left them. I could hear their bellowing as I went up the cliff and for a long time afterward.

Chapter 14

My leg hurt so much by the time I had reached the house that it was hard for me to crawl under the fence and move aside the heavy rock.

For five suns I could not go out because my leg had swollen so badly and I had no herbs with which to treat it. I had enough food to eat, but on the third day the water in the basket ran low. Two days later the basket was empty. It was necessary then for me to go to the spring in the ravine.

I started out when the sun rose. I took with me shellfish to eat, also my spear and my bow and arrows. I went very slowly, for I had to crawl on my hands and knees, carrying the food tied to my back, and dragging the weapons.

There was a short way to the spring, but it was over many rocks which I could not climb, so I had to take a longer way through the brush. I reached the ravine when the sun was overhead. The spring was not far off and I rested there, though I was very thirsty, cutting a lobe from a cactus bush to chew on.

While I was resting there, sucking the juice from the cactus, I saw the big gray dog, the leader of the wild pack, in the brush above me. His head was down and he was moving slowly, sniffing the tracks I had made. He saw me soon after I saw him and stopped. Behind him was the rest of the pack, trotting along one after the other. The pack stopped too.

I took up my bow and fitted an arrow, but as I did this the big dog faded away into the brush and was quickly followed by the others. In the time of one breath they were gone. There was nothing to aim my arrow at. It was as if they had not been there at all.

I listened. They were moving so silently I could not hear their steps, but I was sure that they would try to surround me. Slowly I crawled on, stopping to listen, to glance back, to measure the distance between me and the spring. My leg hurt. I left my bow and arrows behind as I went on, for the brush had grown heavy and I could not use them. In one hand I dragged my spear.

I came to the spring. It flowed out of a crack in a rock and the rock rose high on three sides of it. The wild dogs could not attack me from any of these directions, so I lay on the earth and drank, watching the ravine below me. I drank for a long time and filled my basket and then, feeling better, crawled toward the mouth of the cave.

A ledge of black rock ran out above it. Some low bushes grew there and among them, with just his head showing, stood the big gray dog. He did not move, but his yellow eyes followed me, turning slowly as I drew near the cave. Another head showed behind him and another. They were too far away for me to reach with my spear.

Suddenly I saw brush moving on the opposite bank of the ravine. The pack had split up and were waiting on both sides of the ravine for me to pass them.

The cave was now in front of me. I crawled to the mouth and into it. Above me I could hear feet running and the cracking of brush, which was followed by silence.

I was safe. I knew the wild dogs would come back and they did as night fell, stalking around in the brush until morning, but not venturing close.

Although the mouth of the cave was small, once you were inside, it spread out and you could stand up. Water dropped from the roof and the cave was cold without a fire, but here I stayed for six suns, until my leg was well, crawling out only once to fetch water from the spring.

While I was living there I decided that I would make the cave into another house, where I could stay should I again get hurt or sick. And this I did as soon as I was strong and could walk.

The cave went far back into the hill, around many turns, but I needed only that part which lay near the opening and which the sun could reach during some of the day.

A long time before this my ancestors had used the cave, why I do not know, and along the walls on each side they had cut figures in the stone. There were figures of pelicans floating on the water and flying, of dolphins, whales, sea elephants, gulls, ravens, dogs, and foxes. Near the opening of the cave they had also cut two deep basins in the stone, which I decided to use for storing water since they held much more than the baskets.

I made shelves in the side of the rock as I had done in the other house, and gathered shellfish and seeds to store there. I also gathered herbs from the hill above the spring in case I should need them. The bow and arrows I had first made I likewise took to the cave. At the last, after I had made a good bed of seaweed and collected dry wood for my fires, I closed the opening with stones, except for a small hole at the top which I could crawl through.

All this I did, thinking of the days I had been sick and without water. It was hard work, much of it man's work, but not until I was finished did I go back to the place where the sea elephants lived.

The tide was low when I reached it. Far up on the slope lay the body of the old bull. Gulls had picked his bones clean, but I found what I had come for.

Some of the teeth were as long as my hand and half its width. They were curved at the tops and some were broken, but when I had ground the best of them down with sand, I had for my work four good spear points, broad at the bottom and very sharp at the ends.

I made two more spears from these points and at last was ready to go to the cave of the wild dogs.

Chapter 15

There had been wild dogs on the Island of the Blue Dolphins as long as I remember, but after the Aleuts had slain most of the men of our tribe and their dogs had left to join the others, the pack became much bolder. It spent the nights running through the village and during the day was never far off. It was then that we made plans to get rid of them, but the ship came and everyone left Ghalas-at.

I am sure that the pack grew bolder because of their leader, the big one with the thick fur around his neck and the yellow eyes.

I had never seen this dog before the Aleuts came and no one else had, so he must have come with them and been left behind when they sailed away. He was a much larger dog than any of ours, which besides have short hair and brown eyes. I was sure that he was an Aleut dog.

Already I had killed four of the pack, but there were many left, more than in the beginning, for some had been born in the meantime. The young dogs were even wilder than the old ones.

I first went to the hill near the cave when the pack was away and collected armloads of brush which I placed near the mouth of their lair. Then I waited until the pack was in the cave. It went there early in the morning to sleep after it had spent the night prowling. I took with me the big bow and five arrows and two of the spears. I went quietly circling around the mouth of the cave and came up to it from the side. There I left all of my weapons except one spear.

I set fire to the brush and pushed it into the cave. If the wild dogs heard me, there was no sound from them. Nearby was a ledge of rock which I climbed, taking my weapons with me.

The fire burned high. Some of the smoke trailed out over the hill, but much of it stayed in the cave. Soon the pack would have to leave. I did not hope to kill more than five of them because I had only that many arrows, but if the leader was one of the five I would be satisfied. It might be wiser if I waited and saved all my arrows for him, and this I decided to do.

None of the dogs appeared before the fire died. Then three ran out and away. Seven more followed and a long time afterwards a like number. There were many more still left in the cave.

The leader came next. Unlike the others, he did not run away. He jumped over the ashes and stood at the mouth of the cave, sniffing the air. I was so close to him that I could see his nose quivering, but he did not see me until I raised my bow. Fortunately I did not frighten him.

He stood facing me, his front legs spread as if he were ready to spring, his yellow eyes narrowed to slits. The arrow struck him in the chest. He turned away from me, took one step and fell. I sent another arrow toward him which went wide.

At this time three more dogs trotted out of the cave. I used the last of my arrows and killed two of them.

Carrying both of the spears, I climbed down from the ledge and went through the brush to the place where the leader had fallen. He was not there. While I had been shooting at the other dogs, he had gone. He could not have gone far because of his wound, but though I looked everywhere, around the ledge where I had been standing and in front of the cave, I did not find him.

I waited for a long time and then went inside the cave. It was deep, but I could see clearly.

Far back in a corner was the half-eaten carcass of a fox. Beside it was a black dog with four gray pups. One of the pups came slowly toward me, a round ball of fur that I could have held in my hand. I wanted to hold it, but the mother leaped to her feet and bared her teeth. I raised my spear as I backed out of the cave, yet I did not use it. The wounded leader was not there.

Night was coming and I left the cave, going along the foot of the hill that led to the cliff. I had not gone far on this trail that the wild dogs used when I saw the broken shaft of an arrow. It had been gnawed off near the tip and I knew it was from the arrow which had wounded the leader.

Farther on I saw his tracks in the dust. They were uneven as if he were traveling slowly. I followed them toward the cliff, but finally lost them in the darkness.

The next day and the next it rained and I did not go to look for him. I spent those days making more arrows, and on the third day, with these arrows and my spear, I went out along the trail the wild dogs had made to and from my house.

There were no tracks after the rain, but I followed the trail to the pile of rocks where I had seen them before. On the far side of the rocks I found the big gray dog. He had the broken arrow in his chest and he was lying with one of his legs under him.

He was about ten paces from me so I could see him clearly. I was sure that he was dead, but I lifted the spear and took good aim at him. Just as I was about to throw the spear, he raised his head a little from the earth and then let it drop.

This surprised me greatly and I stood there for a while not knowing what to do, whether to use the spear or my bow. I was used to animals playing dead until they suddenly turned on you or ran away.

The spear was the better of the two weapons at this distance, but I could not use it as well as the other, so I climbed onto the rocks where I could see him if he ran. I placed my feet carefully. I had a second arrow ready should I need it. I fitted an arrow and pulled back the string, aiming at his head.

Why I did not send the arrow I cannot say. I stood on the rock with the bow pulled back and my hand would not let it go. The big dog lay there and did not move and this may be the reason. If he had gotten up I would have killed him. I stood there for a long time looking down at him and then I climbed off the rocks.

He did not move when I went up to him, nor could I see him breathing until I was very close. The head of the arrow was in his chest and the broken shaft was covered with blood. The thick fur around his neck was matted from the rain.

I do not think that he knew I was picking him up, for his body was limp, as if he were dead. He was very heavy and the only way I could lift him was by kneeling and putting his legs around my shoulders.

In this manner, stopping to rest when I was tired, I carried him to the headland.

I could not get through the opening under the fence, so I cut the bindings and lifted out two of the whale ribs and thus took him into the house. He did not look at me or raise his head when I laid him on the floor, but his mouth was open and he was breathing.

The arrow had a small point, which was fortunate, and came out easily though it had gone deep. He did not move while I did this, nor afterwards as I cleaned the wound with a peeled stick from a coral bush. This bush has poisonous berries, yet its wood often heals wounds that nothing else will.

I had not gathered food for many days and the baskets were empty, so I left water for the dog and, after mending the fence, went down to the sea. I had no thought that he would live and I did not care.

All day I was among the rocks gathering shellfish and only once did I think of the wounded dog, my enemy, lying there in the house, and then to wonder why I had not killed him.

He was still alive when I got back, though he had not moved from the place where I had left him. Again I cleaned the wound with a coral twig. I then lifted his head and put water in his mouth, which he swallowed. This was the first time that he had looked at me since the time I had found him on the trail. His eyes were sunken and they looked out at me from far back in his head.

Before I went to sleep I gave him more water. In the morning I left food for him when I went down to the sea, and when I came home he had eaten it. He was lying in the corner, watching me. While I made a fire and cooked my supper, he watched me. His yellow eyes followed me wherever I moved.

That night I slept on the rock, for I was afraid of him, and at dawn as I went out I left the hole under the fence open so he could go. But he was there when I got back, lying in the sun with his head on his paws. I had speared two fish, which I cooked for my supper. Since he was very thin, I gave him one of them, and after he had eaten it he came over and lay down by the fire, watching me with his yellow eyes that were very narrow and slanted up at the corners.

Four nights I slept on the rock, and every morning I left the hole under the fence open so he could leave. Each day I speared a fish for him and when I got home he was always at the fence waiting for it. He would not take the fish from me so I had to put it on the ground. Once I held out my hand to him, but at this he backed away and showed his teeth.

On the fourth day when I came back from the rocks early he was not there at the fence waiting. A strange feeling came over me. Always before when I returned, I had hoped that he would be gone. But now as I crawled under the fence I did not feel the same.

I called out, "Dog, Dog," for I had no other name for him.

I ran toward the house, calling it. He was inside. He was just getting to his feet, stretching himself and yawning. He looked first at the fish I carried and then at me and moved his tail.

That night I stayed in the house. Before I fell asleep I thought of a name for him, for I could not call him Dog. The name I thought of was Rontu, which means in our language Fox Eyes.

Chapter 16

The white men's ship did not return that spring or in the summer. But every day, whether I was on the headland or gathering shellfish on the rocks or working on my canoe, I watched for it. I also watched for the red ship of the Aleuts.

I was not sure what I would do if the Aleuts came. I could hide in the cave which I had stored with food and water, for it was surrounded by thick brush and the mouth of the ravine could only be reached from the sea. The Aleuts had not used the spring and did not know about it because there was another one closer to where they had camped. But they might come upon the cave by chance and then I must be ready to flee.

For this reason I worked on the canoe I had abandoned on the spit. I went to the place where the others were hidden, but they were dried out and cracked. Also they were too heavy for a girl to push into the water, even a girl as strong as I was.

The tides had almost buried the canoe, and I labored many days to dig it out of the sand. Since the weather was warm, I did not go back and forth to my house on the headland, but cooked my meals on the sandspit and at night slept in the canoe, which saved much time.

Even this canoe was too big for me to pull easily in and out of the water, so I set about making it smaller. I did this by loosening all the planks, by cutting the sinews and heating the pitch that bound them together. I then shaped these planks to half their length, using sharp knives made from a black stone which is to be found at one place on the island, and bound them back together with fresh pitch and sinews.

The canoe when I had finshed was not so beautiful as it had been before, but I could now lift one end of it and drag it through the waves.

All the time I was working on the canoe, which was most of that summer, Rontu was with me. He was either sleeping in the shade of the canoe or running up and down the sandspit chasing the pelicans that roost there in great numbers because there are numerous fish nearby. He never caught any of the birds, yet he would keep trying until his tongue hung out of his mouth.

He had learned his name quickly and many words that meant something to him. *Zalwit,* for example, which is our word for pelican, and *naip* which means fish. I talked to him often, using these words and others and many that he did not understand, just as though I were talking to one of my people.

"Rontu," I would say after he had stolen a special fish I had speared for my supper, "tell me why it is that you are such a handsome dog and yet such a thief."

He would put his head on one side and then the other, although he knew only two of the words, and look at me.

Or I would say, "It is a beautiful day. I have never seen the ocean so calm and the sky looks like a blue shell. How long do you think these days will last?"

Rontu would look up at me just the same, though he understood none of the words, acting as if he did.

Because of this I was not lonely. I did not know

how lonely I had been until I had Rontu to talk to.

When the canoe was finished and the pitch had dried I wanted to find out how it went through the water and if the planks leaked, so we set off on a long voyage around the island. The voyage took all of one day, from dawn until night.

There are many sea caves on the Island of the Blue Dolphins and some of them are large and go far back into the cliffs. One of these was near the headland where my house stood.

The opening was narrow, not much wider than the canoe, but once we were inside, it spread out and was larger than my place on the headland.

The walls were black and smooth and slanted far up over my head. The water was almost as black, except where light came through the opening. Here it was a gold color and you could see fish swimming around. They were different from the fish on the reefs, having larger eyes and fins that drifted out from their bodies like kelp.

This place opened into another, which was smaller and so dark I could see nothing. It was very silent in there, with no sound of the waves on the shore and only the lapping of the water against the rocky walls. I thought of the god Tumaiyowit who had become angry at Mukat and gone down, down into another world, and I wondered if it were not to such a place as this that he had gone.

Far ahead was a spot of light no larger than my hand, so instead of turning back, which I felt like doing, I drifted toward it around many turnings and came at last to another room much like the first.

Along one side was a wide shelf of rock, which ran out to the sea through a narrow opening. The tide was full and yet the shelf was out of the water. It was a fine place to hide a canoe, which could be lifted out and stored there where no one could find it. The ledge joined the cliff just below my house. All I needed was a trail down to the cave and then the canoe would be close at hand.

"We have made a great discovery," I said to Rontu.

Rontu did not hear me. He was watching a devilfish, just beyond the opening of the cave. This fish has a small head with eyes that bulge and many arms. All day Rontu had been barking—at the cormorants, the gulls, the seals—at everything that moved. Now he was quiet, watching the black thing in the water.

I let the canoe drift along and knelt down out of sight until I could pick up my spear.

The devilfish was in front of us, swimming slowly near the surface, moving all his arms at once. Large devilfish are dangerous if you are in the sea, for their arms are as long as a man, and they can quickly wrap them around you. They also have a big mouth and a sharp beak where their arms join their head. This one was the largest I had ever seen.

Since Rontu was standing in front of me and I could not put the canoe into a better position, I had to lean out to use the spear. As I did so, the devilfish saw my movement and let loose in the water a black cloud of liquid which instantly hid him from view.

I knew that the devilfish would not be in the center of this cloud, that he had left it behind. I therefore did not aim my spear at it, but picked up the paddle and waited until he appeared. He was now twice the length of the canoe from me and though I paddled fast I could not overtake him.

"Rontu," I said, for he was watching the black

cloud in the water, "you have much to learn about the devilfish."

Rontu did not look at me or bark. He put his head to one side and then the other, still puzzled, more so when the cloud disappeared and nothing was left except clear water.

Devilfish is the best food in the seas. The flesh is white and tender and very sweet. But they are difficult to catch without a special kind of spear, which I now decided to make during the winter when I would have much time.

I took the canoe to Coral Cove, not far from the cave, and pulled it up on the shore out of reach of the winter storms. There it would be safe until spring when I would hide it in the cave that Rontu and I had found. It was easy to paddle and did not leak. I was very happy.

Chapter 17

Storms came early with rain and between the rains fierce winds struck the island and filled the air with sand. During this time, I made myself another dress, but most of the days I spent fashioning a spear to catch the giant devilfish.

I had seen this spear made, as I had seen my father make bows and arrows, yet I knew little about it, no more than I had about the others. Still I remembered how it looked and how it was used. From these memories I made it after many errors and many hours of work, sitting on the floor while Rontu slept nearby and the storms beat upon the roof.

Four of the sea-elephant teeth were left, and though I broke all except one, this I worked down to a head with a barbed point. I then made a ring and fastened it to the end of the shaft, and into this ring fitted the head, which was tied to a long string made of braided sinew. When the spear was thrown and struck a devilfish, the head came loose from the shaft. The shaft floated on the water, but the pointed barb was held by the string which was tied to your wrist. This spear was especially good because it could be thrown from a distance.

On the first day of spring I went down to Coral Cove with my new spear. I knew it was spring because that morning at dawn the sky was filled with flocks of darting birds. They were small and black and came only at this time of year. They came out of the south and stayed for two suns, hunting food in the ravines, and then flew off in one great flight toward the north.

Rontu did not go with me to the beach because I had let him out of the fence and he had not returned. The wild dogs had been to the house many times that winter and he had paid no heed to them, but the night before, after they had come and gone, he had stood at the fence. He stood and whined and walked up and down. It worried me to see him act so strangely, and when he refused to eat I finally let him out.

Now I pushed the canoe into the water and drifted toward the reef where the devilfish lived. The water was so clear that it was like the air around me. Far down, the sea ferns moved as though a breeze were blowing there, and among them swam the devilfish trailing their long arms.

It was good to be on the sea after the winter storms, with the new spear in my hand, but all the morning as I hunted the giant devilfish I kept thinking of Rontu. I should have been happy, yet thinking of him I was not. Would he come back, I wondered, or had he gone to live with the wild dogs? Would he again be my enemy? If he were my enemy, I knew that I could never kill him, now that he had been my friend.

When the sun was high I hid the canoe in the cave we had found, for once more it was the time the Aleuts might return, and with the two small bass I had speared, though not the giant devilfish, I went up the cliff. I had planned to make a trail from the cave to my house, but had decided that it could be seen from a ship and by anyone standing on the headland.

The climb was steep. As I reached the top, I paused for breath. The morning was quiet except for the noise of the little birds flying from bush to bush and the cries of the gulls who did not like these strangers. Then I heard the sound of dogs fighting. The sound came from far off, perhaps from the ravine, and taking my bow and arrows, I hurried in that direction.

I went down the path which led to the spring. There were tracks of the wild dogs around the spring, and among them I saw the large ones of Rontu. The tracks led away through the ravine which winds to the sea. I heard again the distant sound of fighting.

I went slowly through the ravine because of my bow and arrows.

At last I came to the place where it opens into a meadow right at the edge of a low sea cliff. Sometimes in the summers, a long time ago, my people had lived here. They gathered shellfish on the rocks and ate them here, leaving the shells which after many summers had formed a mound. Over this grass had grown, and a thick-leaved plant called *gnapan*.

On this mound, among the grasses and the plants, stood Rontu. He stood facing me, with his back to the sea cliff. In front of him in a half-circle were the wild dogs. At first I thought that the pack had driven him there against the cliff and were getting ready to attack him. But I soon saw that two dogs stood out from the rest of the pack, between it and Rontu, and that their muzzles were wet with blood.

One of these dogs was the leader who had taken Rontu's place when he had come to live with me. The other one, which was spotted, I had never seen. The battle was between Rontu and these two dogs. The rest were there to fall upon whichever was beaten.

So great was the noise made by the pack, they had

not heard me as I came through the brush, nor did they see me now as I stood at the edge of the meadow. They sat on their haunches and barked, with their eyes fixed on the others. But I was sure that Rontu knew I was somewhere near, for he raised his head and smelled the air.

The two dogs were trotting back and forth along the foot of the mound, watching Rontu. The fight had probably started at the spring and they had stalked him to this place where he had chosen to fight.

The sea cliff was behind him and they could not reach him from that direction so they were trying to think of some other way. It would have been easier if one could have attacked him from the back and one from the front.

Rontu did not move from where he stood on top of the mound. Now and again he lowered his head to lick a wound on his leg, but whenever he did he always kept his eyes on the two dogs trotting up and down.

I could have shot them, for they were within reach of my bow, or driven off the pack, yet I stood in the brush and watched. This was a battle between them and Rontu. If I stopped it, they would surely fight again, perhaps at some other place less favorable to him.

Rontu again licked his wound and this time he did not watch the two dogs moving slowly past the mound. I thought it was a lure and so it proved to be, for suddenly they ran toward him. They came from opposite sides of the mound, ears laid back and teeth bared.

Rontu did not wait for the attack, but, leaping at the nearer one, turned his shoulder and with his head lowered caught the dog's foreleg. The pack was quiet.

In the silence, I could hear the sound of the bone breaking, and the dog backed away on three legs.

The spotted dog had reached the top of the mound. Whirling away from the one he had crippled, Rontu faced him, but not in time to fend off the first heavy rush. Teeth slashed at his throat and, as he turned his body, struck him instead on the flank, and he went down.

At that moment, while he lay there on the grass with the dog circling warily and the pack moving slowly toward him, without knowing that I did so, I fitted an arrow to the bow. A good distance separated Rontu from his attacker and I could end the battle before he was wounded further or the pack fell upon him. Yet, as before, I did not send the arrow.

The spotted dog paused, and turned in his tracks, and again leaped, this time from behind.

Rontu was still lying in the grass with his paws under him and I thought he did not see that the other was upon him. But crouching there, he suddenly raised himself and at the same time fastened his teeth in the dog's throat.

Together they rolled off the mound, yet Rontu did not let go. The pack sat restless in the grass.

In a short time Rontu rose to his feet and left the spotted dog where it lay. He walked to the top of the mound and lifted his head and gave a long howl. I had never heard this sound before. It was the sound of many things that I did not understand.

He trotted past me and up the ravine. When I got to the house he was there waiting, as if he had not been away or nothing had happened.

In all the time he lived, Rontu never left again, and the wild dogs, which for some reason divided into two packs, after that never returned to the headland.

Chapter 18

Flowers were plentiful that spring because of the winter's heavy rains. The dunes were covered with mats of sand flowers, which are red and have tiny eyes that are sometimes pink and sometimes white. Yuccas grew tall among the rocks of the ravine. Their heads were clustered with curly globes no larger than pebbles and the color of the sun when it rises. Lupines grew where the springs ran. From the sunny cliffs, in crevices where no one would think anything could grow, sprang the little red and yellow fountains of the comul bush.

Birds were plentiful, too. There were many hummers which can stand still in the air and look like bits of polished stone and have long tongues to sip honey with. There were blue jays, which are very quarrelsome birds, and black-and-white peckers that pecked holes in the yucca stalks and the poles of my roof, even in the whale bones of the fence. Red-winged blackbirds also came flying out of the south, and flocks of crows, and a bird with a yellow body and a scarlet head, which I had never seen before.

A pair of these birds made a nest in a stunted tree near my house. It was made from strings of the yucca bush and had a small opening at the top and hung down like a pouch. The mother laid two speckled eggs which she and her mate took turns sitting on. After the eggs hatched, I put shreds of abalone under the tree and these she fed her young.

The young birds were not like their mother and

father, being gray and very ugly, but anyway, I took them from the nest, and put them in a small cage that I made of reeds. So later in the spring, when all the birds except the crows left the island and flew off to the north, I had these two for friends.

They soon grew beautiful feathers like those of their parents and began to make the same sound, which was *reep, reep*. But it was soft and clear and much sweeter than the cries of the gulls or the crows or the talk of the pelicans which sounds like the quarreling of toothless old men.

Before summer came the cage was too small for my two birds, but instead of building a larger one, I cut the tips of their wings, one wing of each, so they could not fly away, and let them loose in the house. By the time their wings had grown out, they had learned to take food from my hand. They would jump down from the roof and perch on my arm and beg, making their *reep, reep* sound.

When their wings began to feather out, I cut them again. This time I let them loose in the yard, where they hopped around hunting food, perching on Rontu who by now had gotten used to them. The next time they feathered out, I did not trim their wings, but they never flew farther away than the ravine and would always come back at night to sleep and, no matter how much they had eaten, to ask for food.

One, because he was larger, I called Tainor. I named him after a young man I liked who had been killed by the Aleuts. The other was called Lurai, which was a name I wished I had been called instead of Karana.

During the time that I was taming the birds, I made another skirt. This one I also made of yucca fibers softened in water and braided into twine. I made it just like the others, with folds running lengthwise. It was open on both sides and hung to my knees. The belt I made of sealskin which could be tied in a knot. I also made a pair of sandals from sealskin for walking over the dunes when the sun was hot, or just to be dressed up when I wore my new skirt of yucca twine.

Often I would put on the skirt and the sandals and walk along the cliff with Rontu. Sometimes I made a wreath of flowers and fastened it in my hair. After the Aleuts had killed our men at Coral Cove, all the women of our tribe had singed their hair short as a sign of mourning. I had singed mine, too, with a faggot, but now it had grown long again and came to my waist. I parted it and let it fall down my back, except when I wore a wreath. Then I made braids and fastened them with long whalebone pins.

I also made a wreath for Rontu's neck, which he did not like. Together we would walk along the cliff looking at the sea, and though the white men's ship did not return that spring, it was a happy time. The air smelled of flowers and birds sang everywhere.

Chapter 19

Another summer had come and still I had not speared the giant devilfish that lived near the cave.

Every day during the spring, Rontu and I went to look for him. I would put the canoe in the water and paddle slowly through the cave, from one opening to the other, often several times. I saw many devilfish there where the black water is streaked with light, but not the giant one.

At last I gave up looking for him and began to gather abalones for winter. The red shells hold the sweetest meat and are best for drying, though the green ones and the black are also good. Because the red ones are the sweetest, starfish prey upon them.

This star-shaped creature places itself over the shell of an abalone. With its five arms spread out against the rock to which the abalone is fastened, it holds the shell with its suckers, and then begins to lift itself. The starfish pulls against the abalone shell, sometimes for days, holding on with its suckers and pushing up with its legs, until little by little the heavy shell comes loose from the body.

One morning we left the cave and paddled out to the reef which is joined to it.

For many days I had been gathering a few shellfish on the rocks at Coral Cove, but I had been watching the reef and waiting for the right time to harvest. This is when there are few starfish feeding, for they are as hard to pry loose from an abalone as an abalone is to pry from a rock.

The tide was low and the reef rose far out of the water. Along its sides were great numbers of red abalones and very few starfish, so before the sun was high I filled the bottom of the canoe.

The day was windless, and since I had all I could carry, I tied the canoe, and with Rontu following me, climbed onto the reef to look for fish to spear for our supper.

Blue dolphins were leaping beyond the kelp beds. In the kelp otter were playing at the games they never tire of. And around me everywhere the gulls were fishing for scallops, which were numerous that summer. They grow on the floating kelp leaves and there were so many of them that much of the kelp near the reef had been dragged to the bottom. Still there were scallops that the gulls could reach, and taking them in their beaks they would fly far above the reef and let them drop. The gulls would then swoop down to the rocks and pick the meat from the broken shells.

Scallops fell on the reef like rain, which amused me, but not Rontu who could not understand what the gulls were doing. Dodging this way and that I went to the end of the reef where the biggest fish live. With a sinew line and a hook made of abalone shell I caught two that had large heads and long teeth, but are good to eat. I gave one to Rontu and on the way back to the canoe gathered purple sea urchins to use for dyeing.

Rontu, who was trotting along in front of me, suddenly dropped his fish and stood looking down over the edge of the reef.

There, swimming in the clear water, was a devilfish. It was the same one I had been hunting for. It was the giant!

Seldom did you see any devilfish here, for they like deep places, and the water along this part of the reef is shallow. Perhaps this one lived in the cave and came here only when he could not find food.

Rontu made no sound. I fixed the head of the spear and the long string that held it to my wrist. I then crawled back to the edge of the reef.

The giant had not moved. He was floating just below the surface of the water and I could plainly see his eyes. They were the size of small stones and stood out from his head, with black rims and gold centers and in the centers a black spot, like the eyes of a spirit I had once seen on a night that rain fell and lightning forked in the sky.

Where my hands rested was a deep crevice and in it a fish was hiding.

The giant was half the length of my spear from the reef, but while I watched, one of his long arms ran out like a snake and felt its way into the crevice. It went past the fish and along the side of the rock and then the end of it curled back. As the arm gently wound itself around the fish from behind, I rose to one knee and drove the spear.

I aimed at the giant's head, but though it was larger than my two fishes and a good target, I missed. The spear struck down through the water and slanted off. Instantly a black cloud surrounded the devilfish. The only thing I could see of him was one long arm still grasping his prey.

I jumped to my feet to pull in the spear, thinking that I might have a chance to throw it again. As I did so, the shaft bobbed back to the surface and I saw that the barbed point had come loose.

At the same moment the string tightened. My grip on it broke, and aware that I had struck the devilfish,

I quickly dropped the coils I held, for when the string runs out fast it burns your hands or becomes entangled.

The devilfish does not swim with fins or flippers, like other things in the sea. He takes water in through the hole in the front of his body and pushes the water out behind through two slits. When he is swimming slowly you can see these two streams trailing out, but only then. When he moves fast, you can see nothing except a streak in the water.

The coils I had dropped on the rock hopped and sang as they ran. Then there were no more of them. The string tightened on my wrist and, to lessen the shock, I leaped across the crevice in the direction the giant had taken. With the string in both hands, but still fastened to my wrist, I braced my feet on the slippery rock and leaned backwards.

The string snapped tight with the weight of the devilfish. It began to stretch, and fearing that it might break, I walked forward, yet I made him pull me every step.

He was moving toward the cave, along the edge of the reef. The cave was a good distance away. If he got there I would surely lose him. The canoe was tied just in front of me. Once I was in it, I could let him pull me until he grew tired. But there was no way to untie the canoe and still hold on to the string.

Rontu all this time was running up and down the reef barking and leaping at me, which made my task harder.

Step by step I walked forward, until the devilfish was in the deep water close to the cave. He was so close that I had to stop, even if the sinew broke and I lost him. I therefore braced myself and did not move. The sinew stretched, throwing off drops of water. I could hear it stretch and I was sure it would break. I did not feel it cutting into my hands, though they bled.

The pull suddenly lessened and I was sure that he was gone, but the next instant I saw the string cutting the water in a wide circle. He was swimming off from the cave and the reef toward some rocks that were about twice the length of the string away. He would be safe there, too, for among them were many places to hide.

I pulled in half the string while he was moving toward the rocks, but soon had to let it out. It grew tight and again began to stretch. The water here was only a little over my waist, and I let myself down over the reef.

There was a sand bar not far from the rocks, and stepping carefully on the bottom, which was full of holes, I slowly made my way toward it. Rontu swam along by my side.

I reached the sand bar before the devilfish could hide himself in the rocks. The string held and he turned about and once more swam toward the cave. Twice again he did this. Each time I took in some of the string. The third time, as he came up into the shallow water, I walked backward across the sand bar so he would not see me, and pulled on the string with all my strength.

The giant slid up on the sand. He lay with his arms spread out, partly in the water, and I thought he was dead. Then I saw his eyes moving. Before I could shout a warning, Rontu had rushed forward and seized him. But the devilfish was too heavy to lift or shake. As Rontu's jaws sought another hold, three of the many arms wound themselves around his neck.

Devilfish are only dangerous when in the water

where they can fasten themselves to you with their long arms. These arms have rows of suckers underneath them and they can drag you under and hold you there until you drown. But even on land the devilfish can injure you, for he is strong and does not die quickly.

The giant was flailing his arms, struggling to get back into the water. Little by little he was dragging Rontu with him. I could no longer use the string because it was wound around Rontu's legs.

The whalebone knife I used for prying abalones from the rocks was tied to a thong at my waist. The blade was thick at the point but had a sharp edge. I dropped the coils of string and unfastened the knife as I ran.

I ran past the devilfish and got between him and the deep water. So many of his arms were flailing that it was useless to cut any one of them. One struck me on the leg and burned like a whip. Another, which Rontu had chewed off, lay wriggling at the edge of the water, as if it were looking for something to fasten on to.

The head rose out of the twisting arms like a giant stalk. The gold eyes with their black rims were fixed on me. Above the sounds of the waves and the water splashing and Rontu's barking, I could hear the snapping of his beak, which was sharper than the knife I held in my hand.

I drove the knife down into his body and as I did this I was suddenly covered, or so it seemed, with a countless number of leeches, sucking at my skin. Fortunately one hand was free, the hand that held the knife, and again and again I struck down through the tough hide. The suckers, which were fastened to me and pained greatly, lessened their hold. Slowly the arms stopped moving and then grew limp.

I tried to drag the devilfish out of the water, but my strength was gone. I did not even go back to the reef for my canoe, though I did take the shaft and the head of the spear, which had cost me much labor, and the sinew line.

It was night before Rontu and I got back to the house.

Rontu had a gash on his nose from the giant's beak, and I had many cuts and bruises. I saw two more giant devilfish along the reef that summer, but I did not try to spear them.

Chapter 20

I gathered two more canoeloads of abalones soon after that, mostly the sweet red ones, which I cleaned and carried to the house. Along the south part of the fence where the sun shone most of the day, I built long shelves out of branches and put the meat up to dry. Abalones are larger than your hand and twice as thick when fresh, but they shrink small in the sun so you have to dry many.

In the old days on the island there were children to keep away the gulls, which would rather feast on abalones than anything else. In one morning, if the meat was left unguarded, they could fly off with a month's harvest.

At first, whenever I went to the spring or to the beach, I left Rontu behind to chase them off, but he did not like this and howled all the time I was gone. Finally I tied strings to some of the abalone shells and hung them from poles. The insides of the shells are bright and catch the sun and they turn one way and another in the wind. After that I had little trouble with the gulls.

I also caught small fish in a net I had made and hung them up to dry for winter light. With meat drying on the shelves and the shells flashing and turning in the wind and the strings of fish hanging on the fence, the yard looked as if a whole village were living there on the headland instead of just Rontu and me.

Every morning after I had gathered food for

winter, we went out on the sea. At the end of summer I would gather roots and seeds to store, but now there was nothing that needed to be done. We went many places those first days of summer—to the beach where the sea elephants lived, to Black Cave which was even larger than the first cave we found, and to Tall Rock where the cormorants roosted.

Tall Rock was more than a league from the island and was black and shimmering because it was covered with cormorants. I killed ten of the birds the first time we went there and I skinned and fleshed them and put them out to dry, for someday I wanted to make myself a skirt of cormorant feathers.

Black Cave was on the south coast of the island, near the place where the canoes were stored. In front of the cave was a high ledge of rocks surrounded by deep kelp beds, and I would have paddled by it if I had not seen a sea hawk fly out. The sun was in the west and I had a long way to go to reach home, but I was curious about the hawk and the place he lived in.

The opening of the cave was small, like the one in the cave under the headland, and Rontu and I had to crouch low to get through. Weak light came from outside and I saw that we were in a room with black, shining walls that curved high overhead. At the far end of the room was another small opening. It was long and very dark, but when we reached the end of it we were in another room which was larger than the first and lit with a shaft of light. The light came from the sun, which shone down through a jagged crack in the ceiling.

Seeing the sun shining down and the black shadows drifting over the walls, Rontu barked, then began to howl. The sound echoed through the cave like the howling of a whole pack of dogs. It sent a cold feeling down my back.

"Be quiet!" I shouted, putting my hand over his jaws. My words echoed and echoed in the room.

I turned the canoe around and started back toward the opening. Above it, on a deep ledge that ran from one side of the room to the other, my gaze fell upon a row of strange figures. There must have been two dozen of them standing against the black wall. They were as tall as I, with long arms and legs and short bodies made of reeds and clothed in gull feathers. Each one had eyes fashioned of round or oblong disks of abalone shell, but the rest of their faces were blank. The eyes glittered down at me, moved as the light on the water moved and was reflected upon them. They were more alive than the eyes of those who live.

In the middle of the group was a seated figure, a skeleton. It sat leaning against the wall with its knees drawn up and in its fingers, which were raised to its mouth, a flute of pelican bone.

There were other things there on the ledge, in the shadows among the standing figures, but having drifted far back in the room, I again paddled toward the opening. I had forgotten that the tide was coming in. To my great surprise the opening had narrowed. It was too small now for me to get through. We would have to stay there in the room until the tide went out, until dawn came.

I paddled to the far end of the cave. I did not look back at the glittering eyes of the figures on the ledge. I crouched in the bottom of the canoe and watched the shaft of light grow weak. The opening out to the sea grew smaller and finally disappeared. Night came and a star showed through the crevice overhead.

This star passed out of sight and another took its place. The tide lifted the canoe higher in the room, and as the water lapped against the walls it sounded like the soft music of a flute. It played many tunes through the long night and I slept little, watching the stars change. I knew that the skeleton who sat on the ledge playing his flute was one of my ancestors, and the others with the glittering eyes, though only images, were too, but still I was sleepless and afraid.

With the first light, another high tide almost setting, we left the cave. I did not look up at those standing quietly on the ledge or at the flute player playing for them, but paddled fast out into the morning sea. Nor did I look back.

"I suppose this cave once had a name," I said to Rontu, who was as glad to be free as I was, "but I have never heard of it or heard it spoken about. We will call it Black Cave and never in all our days go there again."

When we came back from our voyage to Tall Rock, I hid the canoe in the cave below the headland. It was hard work, but each time I would lift the canoe from the water and onto the ledge, even though I planned to go out the next morning.

Two summers had come and gone and the Aleut hunters had not returned, yet during these days I always looked for them. At dawn, as Rontu and I went down the cliff, I would watch the ocean for their sails. The summer air was clear and I could see many leagues. Wherever we went in the canoe I would never be gone longer than half a day. On the way home, I always paddled close to shore and looked for them.

It was the last time that we went to Tall Rock that the Aleuts came.

I had hidden the canoe and climbed the cliff with the ten cormorant skins slung over my back. At the top of the cliff I stood for a while gazing at the sea.

There were some small clouds on the water. One of them, the smallest, did not look like the others and as I watched, I saw that it was a ship.

The sun made bright scales on the water, but I could see clearly. There were two sails and it was a ship coming toward the island. For a long time I could not tell the color of the sails. I wondered if it could be the white men, though now I thought about them little and seldom looked for them.

I left the cormorants hanging on the fence and went to the rock on the headland. I could see no better from the rock because the sun was low and the whole ocean was covered with light. Then as I stood there I remembered that the white men's ship would come from the east. This one had come from a different direction—from the north.

I still was not sure that it belonged to the Aleuts, but I decided to pack the things that I would take to the cave in the ravine. There was much to take—my two birds, the skirt I had made, the stone utensils, my beads and earrings, the cormorant feathers, and all of my baskets and weapons. The abalones were not yet dry so I would have to leave them.

When I had packed everything and put it beside the hole under the fence, I went back to the headland. I lay on the rock so I would not be seen and peered over its rim toward the north. For a moment I did not find the ship, and then I saw that it had traveled faster than I thought it would. It was already rounding the kelp bed, close to the rocks of Coral Cove. The last of the sun shone on the ship, on the bow, which was made like the beak of a bird, and on the two red sails.

I knew that the Aleuts would not come on shore in the dark, and that I had until morning to carry my things to the cave, but I did not wait. Most of the night I worked, making two trips to the cave. At dawn, when everything had been moved, I went back to the house for the last time. There I buried the ashes of my fires and threw sand over the shelves and the floor. I took down the shells I had put up to scare the gulls and tossed them and the abalones over the cliff. At last, with a pelican wing, I brushed away the marks of my feet. When I had finished, it looked as though no one had lived there for a long time.

By now the sun was up and I climbed onto the rock. The ship lay at anchor in the cove. Canoes were bringing goods to the shore and some were out in the kelp beds, beginning to hunt for otter. There was a fire on the shore and beside it, a girl. She was cooking something and I could see the fire shining on her hair.

I did not stay long on the headland. Always in the past I had gone to the ravine by a different way so as not to wear a trail. This time I went off toward the west, along the cliff, and then doubled back through the brush, being careful to leave no tracks. Rontu's prints did not matter because the Aleuts knew that there were dogs on the island.

The cave was very dark and I had trouble getting Rontu to go through the small opening. Only after I had crawled in and out several times would he follow me. I closed the opening with stones, and since I was tired, lay down and slept all that day. I slept until I could see the stars shining between the cracks in the rocks.

Chapter 21

I did not take Rontu with me when I left the cave that night. And I closed the opening so that he would not follow me, for if the Aleuts had brought their dogs, he would surely smell them out. I went quietly through the brush to the headland.

Before I had climbed to the top of the high rock I could see the glow of the Aleut fires. They had camped on the mesa, at the place and the spring they had used before. It was less than half a league from my cave.

I stood for a long time watching the fires, wondering if I should move to another part of the island, perhaps to the cave where the wild dogs had lived. I was not afraid that the men would discover me, because they worked on the beach or hunted in their canoes all day. It was the girl I was afraid of. The ravine was tangled with brush, which was hard to walk through, but in the ravine grew seeds and roots. Sometime when she was out looking for food she might wander by the spring and see that it was being used and find my steps leading to the cave.

I stood on the rock until the Aleut fires died. I thought of everything I could do, of the different place I could go, and at last decided to stay in the ravine. The far end of the island had no springs, and if I moved there I would have no place to hide the canoe which I might need.

I went back to the cave and did not leave it until the moon was full. There was little food left. Rontu and I climbed to the headland and when we passed the house I saw that three of the whale ribs had been cut from the fence. No one was there or else Rontu would have barked. I waited until the tide was low, which was close to dawn, and filled a basket with sea water and abalones. We were back in the cave before it grew light.

The sea water kept the abalones fresh, but when we had to go out again the night was too dark to find our way to the reef. I therefore had to gather roots. I could never gather many before the sun rose, so I went out every morning until the next moon came. Then I went to the reef for abalones.

During all this time I saw none of the Aleuts. Nor did the girl come near the cave, though I found her footsteps far down the ravine where she had been to dig roots. The Aleuts had not brought their dogs, which was fortunate, for they would have found Rontu's tracks and followed us to the cave.

The days were long for Rontu and me. At first he would pace up and down the cave and stand at the opening sniffing through the cracks. I did not let him out except when I was with him for fear he would go to the camp and not come back. After a while he got used to this and would lie all day and watch whatever I was doing.

It was dark in the cave, even when the sun was high, so I burned the small fish I had stored. By their light I began to make a cormorant skirt, working every day on it. The ten skins I had taken at Tall Rock were now dry and in condition to sew. All of them were from male cormorants whose feathers are thicker than those of the females and much glossier. The skirt of yucca fibers was simple to make. I wanted this one to be better, so I cut the skins carefully and sewed them with great care.

I made the bottom first, putting the skins end to end, and using three of them. For the rest of the skirt I sewed the others along their sides so that the feathers ran one way on the upper part and a different way along the bottom.

It was a beautiful skirt and I finished it on the day after the second moon. I had burned all of the little fish, and since I could catch no more until the Aleuts left, I took the skirt outside to work on it there. I had found footsteps in the ravine twice again after the first time, but no closer to the cave. I had begun to feel safe, for the winter storms would soon be here and the Aleuts would leave. Before another moon they would be gone.

I had never seen the skirt in the sunlight. It was black, but underneath were green and gold colors, and all the feathers shimmered as though they were on fire. It was more beautiful than I had thought it would be. I worked fast now that it was almost finished, yet from time to time I would stop to hold it against my waist.

"Rontu," I said, feeling giddy with happiness, "if you were not a male dog I would make you one too, as beautiful as this."

Rontu, who was sprawled out at the mouth of the cave, raised his head and yawned at me and went back to sleep.

I was standing in the sunlight, holding the skirt to my waist, when Rontu leaped to his feet. I heard the sound of steps. It came from the direction of the spring and as I turned quickly I saw a girl looking down at me from the brush.

My spear stood beside the mouth of the cave within easy reach. The girl was not more than ten paces from me and with one movement I could have picked up the spear and thrown it. Why I did not throw the spear, I do not know, for she was one of the Aleuts who had killed my people on the beach of Coral Cove.

She said something and Rontu left the mouth of the cave and walked slowly toward her. The hair raised on his neck, but then he walked to where she stood and let her touch him.

The girl looked at me and made a motion with her hands which I took to mean that Rontu was hers.

"No," I cried and shook my head.

I picked up my spear.

She started to turn and I thought that she was going to flee back through the brush. She made another motion which I took to mean that Rontu was now mine. I did not believe her. I held the spear over my shoulder, ready to throw.

"Tutok," she said, pointing to herself.

I did not say my name. I called Rontu and he came back.

The girl looked at him and then at me and smiled. She was older than I, but not so tall. She had a broad face and small eyes that were very black. When she smiled, I saw that her teeth were worn down from chewing seal sinew, but they were very white.

I was still holding the cormorant skirt and the girl pointed to it and said something. There was one word—*wintscha*—which sounded like a word that means pretty in our language.

I was so proud of the skirt that I did not think. The spear was in my hand, but I held up the skirt so the sunlight could shine on all of it.

The girl jumped down from the ledge and came over to me and touched it.

"*Wintscha*," she said again.

I did not say the word, but she wanted to hold the skirt and I gave it to her. She put it against her waist and let it fall from her hips, turning one way and the other. She was graceful and the skirt flowed around her like water, but I hated the Aleuts and took it from her.

"*Wintscha*," she said.

I had not heard words spoken for so long that they sounded strange to me, yet they were good to hear, even though it was an enemy who spoke them.

She said other words I did not understand, but now as she spoke she looked over my shoulder toward the cave. She pointed to the cave and then to me and made gestures as if she were making a fire. I knew what she wanted me to say, but I did not say it. She wished to know if I lived there in the cave so she could come back with the men and take me to their camp. I shook my head, and pointed to the far end of the island, away, away, for I did not trust her.

She kept looking toward the cave, but she said nothing more about it. I held the spear, which I could have thrown. I did not, though I feared she would return with the hunters.

She came over to me and touched my arm. I did not like the feel of her hand. She said more words and smiled again and walked to the spring and drank. The next moment she had disappeared in the brush. Rontu did not try to follow her. She made no noise as she went.

I crawled back in the cave and began to pack the things I owned. I had all the day to do it, because the men were working and would not return to their camp before night.

By nightfall I was ready to go. I planned to take my canoe and go to the west part of the island. I could sleep there on the rocks until the Aleuts left, moving from place to place if I needed to.

I carried five baskets up the ravine and hid them

near my house. It was getting dark and I had to go back to the cave for two that were left. Carefully I crawled through the brush and stopped just above the mouth of the cave and listened. Rontu was beside me and he listened also. No one could go through the brush in the dusk without making a sound, except someone who had lived in it for a long time.

I went past the spring and waited and then on to the cave. I felt that someone had been there while I had been away. They could be hiding in the dark watching me. They were waiting until I went into the cave.

I was afraid so I did not go in, but quickly turned around. As I did so I saw something in front of the cave, on the flat rock I used for a step. It was a necklace of black stones of a kind I had never seen.

Chapter 22

I did not go into the cave nor did I take the necklace from the rock. That night I slept on the headland at the place where I had left my baskets. At dawn I went back to the ravine. There I hid myself on a brushy ledge. It was near the spring and from it I could see the mouth of the cave.

The sun rose and shone through the ravine. I could see the necklace lying on the rock. The stones looked blacker than they had in the darkness and there were many of them. I wanted to go down to the cave and count them, to see if they would make two loops around my neck, but I did not leave the ledge.

I stayed there all the morning. The sun was high when Rontu barked and I heard steps below me. The girl came out of the brush singing. She walked to the cave, but when she saw the necklace lying on the rock she grew quiet. She picked up the necklace and put it down again and peered into the mouth of the cave. Two of my baskets were still there. Then she went and drank from the spring and started off through the brush.

I jumped to my feet. "Tutok," I cried, running down the ravine. "Tutok."

She came out of the brush so quickly that she must have been waiting nearby to see if I would return.

I ran to the rock and put on the necklace and turned around for her to admire it. The beads made not two loops but three. They were long and oval instead of round, which is a very hard shape to make and takes much skill.

"Wintscha," she said.

"Wintscha," I said, after her, the word strange on my tongue. Then I said the word that meant pretty in our language.

"Win-tai," she said and laughed, because this was strange to her.

She touched the necklace, giving the word for it, and I gave mine. We pointed out other things—the spring, the cave, a gull flying, the sun and the sky, Rontu asleep—trading the names for them and laughing because they were so different. We sat there on the rock until the sun was in the west and played this game. Then Tutok rose and made a gesture of farewell.

"Mah-nay," she said and waited to hear my name.

"Won-a-pa-lei," I answered, which as I have said, means The Girl with the Long Black Hair. I did not tell her my secret name.

"Mah-nay, Won-a-pa-lei," she said.

"Pah-say-no, Tutok," I replied.

I watched her go through the brush. I stood for a long time listening to her footsteps, until I could hear them no more, and then I went to the headland and brought the baskets back to the cave.

Tutok came again the next day. We sat on the rock in the bright sun, trading words and laughing. The sun went fast in the sky. The time came soon when she had to leave, but she returned on the day that followed. It was on this day, when she was leaving, that I told her my secret name.

"Karana," I said, pointing to myself.

She repeated the word, but she did not understand what it meant.

"Won-a-pa-lei," she said, frowning.

I shook my head. Pointing again to myself, I said, "Karana."

Her black eyes opened wide. Slowly she began to smile.

"*Pah-say-no*, Karana," she said.

That night I began to make a gift for her, in return for the necklace she had given me. At first I thought I would give her a pair of my bone earrings, but remembering that her ears were not pierced and that I had a basket of abalone shells already flaked into thin disks, I set about making a circlet for her hair. I bored two holes in each of the disks, using thorns and fine sand. Between them I put ten olivella shells, which were no larger than the tip of my little finger, and threaded them all together with sinew.

I worked five nights on the circlet and on the fifth day when she came I gave it to her, putting it around her head and tying it in the back.

"*Wintscha,*" she said and hugged me. She was so pleased that I forgot how sore my fingers were from boring the holes in the hard shells.

Many times she came to the cave, and then one morning she did not come. I waited for her all that day and at dusk I left the cave and went to the ledge where I could watch the ravine, fearing that the men had learned that I lived here and would find me. That night I slept on the ledge. The night was cold with the first wind of winter.

Tutok did not return the next day and I remembered that it was near the time when the Aleut hunters would leave. Perhaps they had already gone. That afternoon I went to the headland. I climbed the rock and crawled across it until I could look over the rim. My heart beat loud.

The Aleut ship was still there, but men were working on the deck and canoes were going back and forth. The wind blew hard and few bales of otter skins lay on the shore so probably the ship would leave at dawn.

It was dark when I got back to the ravine. Since the wind was very cold and I was no longer afraid that the Aleuts would find me, I made a fire in the cave and cooked a supper of shellfish and roots. I cooked enough for Rontu and me and for Tutok. I knew Tutok would not come, yet I put her food beside the fire and waited.

Once Rontu barked and I thought I heard the sound of footsteps and went to the opening and listened. I waited a long while and did not eat. Clouds moved from the north, covering the cold sky. The wind grew louder and made wild noises in the ravine. At last I closed the mouth of the cave with stones.

At dawn I went to the headland. The wind had died. Fog lay over the sea, washing against the island in gray waves. I waited a long time for a glimpse of Coral Cove, and finally the sun burned away the fog. The little harbor was deserted. The Aleut ship with its red-beaked prow and red sails had gone.

At first, knowing that I could now leave the cave and move back into my house on the headland, I was happy. But as I stood there on the high rock looking down at the deserted harbor and the empty sea, I began to think of Tutok. I thought of all the times we had sat in the sun together. I could hear her voice and see her black eyes squinting closed when she laughed.

Below me, Rontu was running along the cliff, barking at the screaming gulls. Pelicans were chattering as they fished the blue water. Far off I could hear the bellow of a sea elephant. But suddenly, as I thought of Tutok, the island seemed very quiet.

Chapter 23

The hunters left many wounded otter behind them. Some floated in and died on the shore and others I killed with my spear since they were suffering and could not live. But I found a younger otter that was not badly hurt.

It lay in a bed of bull kelp and I would have paddled by if Rontu had not barked. A strand of kelp was wound around its body and I thought it was sleeping, for often before they go to sleep they anchor themselves in this way to keep from drifting off. Then I saw there was a deep gash across its back.

The otter did not try to swim away as I drew near and reached over the side of the canoe. They have large eyes, especially when they are young, but this one's were so large from fear and pain that I could see my reflection in them. I cut the kelp that held it and took it to a tide pool behind the reef, which was sheltered from the waves.

The day was calm after the storm and I caught two fish along the reef. I was careful to keep them alive, because otter will not eat anything that is dead, and left them in the pool. This was early in the morning.

That afternoon I went back to the pool. The fish had disappeared and the young otter was asleep, floating on its back. I did not try to treat its wound with herbs because salt water heals and the herbs would have washed off anyway.

I brought two fish every day and left them in the pool. The otter would not eat while I was watching.

Then I brought four fish and these also disappeared and finally six, which seemed to be the right number. I brought them whether the day was calm or stormy.

The otter grew and its wound began to heal, but still it stayed in the pool, and now when I came it would be waiting for me and would take the fish from my hand. The pool was not big and it could easily have gotten out and away into the sea, yet it stayed there and slept or waited for me to come with food.

The young otter now was the length of my arm and very glossy. It had a long nose that came to a point and many whiskers on each side and the largest eyes I have ever seen. They would watch me all the time I was at the pool, following me whatever I did, and when I said something, they would move around in a very funny way. In a way, too, that made pain come to my throat because they were gay and sad also.

For a long time I called it Otter as I had called Rontu, Dog. Then I decided to give the otter a name. The name was Mon-a-nee, which means Little Boy with Large Eyes.

It was a hard task catching fish every day, especially if the wind was blowing and the waves were high. Once when I could catch only two and dropped them into the pool, Mon-a-nee ate them quickly and waited for more. When he found that was all I had he swam around in circles, looking at me reproachfully.

The waves were so high the next day that I could not fish on the reef even at low tide, and since I had nothing to give him I did not go to the pool.

It was three days before I could catch fish and when I went there again the pool was deserted. I knew that he would leave someday, but I felt bad that he had gone back to the sea and that I would never catch fish for him again. Nor would I know him if I saw him again in the kelp, for now that he had grown and his wound had healed, he looked like all the others.

Soon after the Aleuts had left I moved back to the headland.

Nothing had been harmed except the fence, which I mended, and in a few days the house was the same as before. The only thing that worried me was that all the abalones I had gathered in the summer were gone. I would need to live from day to day on what I could catch, trying to get enough on the days when I could fish to last through the times when I could not. Through the first part of the winter, before Mon-a-nee swam away, this was sometimes hard to do. Afterwards it was not so hard and Rontu and I always had enough to eat.

While the Aleuts were on the island, I had no chance to catch little smelt and dry them, so the nights that winter were dark and I went to bed early and worked only during the day. But still I made another string for my fishing spear, many hooks of abalone shell, and last of all earrings to match the necklace Tutok had given me.

These took a long time, for I searched the beach many mornings when the tide was out before I found two pebbles of the same color as the stones in the necklace and soft enough to cut. The holes in the earrings took even more time, for the stones were hard to hold, but when I was done and had rubbed them bright in fine sand and water, and fastened them with bone hooks to fit my ears, they were very pretty.

On sunny days I would wear them with my cormorant dress and the necklace, and walk along the cliff with Rontu.

I often thought of Tutok, but on these days especially I would look off into the north and wish that she were here to see me. I could hear her talking in her strange language and I would make up things to say to her and things for her to say to me.

Chapter 24

Spring again was a time of flowers and water ran in the ravines and flowed down to the sea. Many birds came back to the island.

Tainor and Lurai built a nest in the tree where they were born. They built it of dry seaweed and leaves and also with hairs off Rontu's back. Whenever he was in the yard while it was being made, they would swoop down if he were not looking and snatch a beakful of fur and fly away. This he did not like and he finally hid from them until the nest was finished.

I had been right in giving a girl's name to Lurai, for she laid speckled eggs and, with some help from her mate, hatched two ugly fledglings which soon became beautiful. I made up names for them and clipped their wings and before long they were as tame as their parents.

I also found a young gull that had fallen from its nest to the beach below. Gulls make their nests high on the cliffs, in hollow places on the rocks. These places are usually small and often I had watched a young one teetering on the edge of the nest and wondered why it did not fall. They seldom did.

This one, which was white with a yellow beak, was not badly hurt, but he had a broken leg. I took him back to the house and bound the bones together with two small sticks and sinew. For a while he did not try to walk. Then, because he was not old enough to fly, he began to hobble around the yard.

With the young birds and the old ones, the white

gull and Rontu, who was always trotting at my heels, the yard seemed a happy place. If only I had not remembered Tutok. If only I had not wondered about my sister Ulape, where she was, and if the marks she had drawn upon her cheeks had proved magical. If they had, she was now married to Kimko and was the mother of many children. She would have smiled to see all of mine, which were so different from the ones I always wished to have.

Early that spring I started to gather abalones and I gathered many, taking them to the headland to dry. I wanted to have a good supply ready if the Aleuts came again.

One day when I was on the reef filling my canoe, I saw a herd of otter in the kelp nearby. They were chasing each other, putting their heads through the kelp and then going under and coming up again in a different place. It was like a game we used to play in the brush when there were children on the island. I looked for Mon-a-nee, but each of them was like the other.

I filled my canoe with abalones and paddled toward shore, one of the otter following me. As I stopped he dived and came up in front of me. He was far away, yet even then I knew who it was. I never thought that I would be able to tell him from the others, but I was sure it was Mon-a-nee that I held up one of the fish I had caught.

Otter swim very fast and before I could take a breath, he had snatched it from my hand.

For two moons I did not see him and then one morning while I was fishing he came suddenly out of the kelp. Behind him were two baby otter. They were about the size of puppies and they moved along so slowly that from time to time Mon-a-nee had to urge them on. Sea otter cannot swim when they are first born, and have to hold on to their mother. Little by little she teaches her babies by brushing them away with her flippers, then swimming around them in circles until they learn to follow.

Mon-a-nee came close to the reef and I threw a fish into the water. He did not snatch it as he usually did, but waited to see what the young otter would do. When they seemed more interested in me than in food, and the fish started to swim away, he seized it with his sharp teeth and tossed it in front of them.

I threw another fish into the water for Mon-a-nee but he did the same thing as before. Still the babies would not take the food, and at last, tired of playing with it, swam over and began to nuzzle him.

Only then did I know that Mon-a-nee was their mother. Otter mate for life and if the mother dies the father will often raise the babies as best he can. This is what I thought had happened to Mon-a-nee.

I looked down at the little family swimming beside the reef. "Mon-a-nee," I said, "I am going to give you a new name. It is Won-a-nee, which fits you because it means Girl with the Large Eyes."

The young otter grew fast and soon were taking fish from my hand, but Won-a-nee liked abalones better. She would let the abalone I tossed her sink to the bottom and then dive and come up holding it against her body, with a rock held in her mouth. Then she would float on her back and put the abalone on her breast and strike it again and again with the rock until the shell was broken.

She taught her young to do this and sometimes I sat on the reef all the morning and watched the three of them pounding the hard shells against their breasts. If all otters did not eat abalones this way I would have thought it was a game played by Won-a-nee just to please me. But they all did and I always wondered about it, and I wonder to this time.

After that summer, after being friends with Won-a-nee and her young, I never killed another otter. I had an otter cape for my shoulders, which I used until it wore out, but never again did I make a new one. Nor did I ever kill another cormorant for its beautiful feathers, though they have long, thin necks and make ugly sounds when they talk to each other. Nor did I kill seals for their sinews, using instead kelp to bind the things that needed it. Nor did I kill another wild dog, nor did I try to spear another sea elephant.

Ulape would have laughed at me, and others would have laughed, too—my father most of all. Yet this is the way I felt about the animals who had become my friends and those who were not, but in time could be. If Ulape and my father had come back and laughed, and all the others had come back and laughed, still I would have felt the same way, for animals and birds are like people, too, though they do not talk the same or do the same things. Without them the earth would be an unhappy place.

Chapter 25

The Aleuts never again came to the Island of the Blue Dolphins, but every summer I watched for them, and early every spring I gathered shellfish, which I dried and stored in the cave where I kept my canoe.

Two winters after they left I made more weapons— a spear, a bow, and a quiver of arrows. These I also stored in the place beneath the headland, so if the hunters returned I would be ready to go to another part of the island, to move from cave to cave, living in my canoe if necessary.

For many summers after the Aleuts had gone the herd of otter left Coral Cove. The old otter which had survived the Aleut spear and by now were aware that summer was a time of danger would lead the herd away. They went far off to the kelp beds of Tall Rock where they stayed until the first storms of winter.

Often Rontu and I would go to the rock and live there for several days catching fish for Won-a-nee and the others I had come to know.

One summer the otter did not leave, the summer that Rontu died, and I knew then that none of the otter who remembered the hunters were left. Nor did I think of them often nor of the white men who had said they would come back, but did not come.

Until that summer, I had kept count of all the moons since the time my brother and I were alone upon the island. For each one that came and went I cut a mark in a pole beside the door of my house.

There were many marks, from the roof to the floor. But after that summer I did not cut them any more. The passing of the moons now had come to mean little, and I only made marks to count the four seasons of the year. The last year I did not count those.

It was late in the summer that Rontu died. The days since spring, whenever I went to the reef to fish, he would not go with me unless I urged him to. He liked to lie in the sun in front of the house and I let him, but I did not go so often as in the past.

I remember the night that Rontu stood at the fence and barked for me to let him out. Usually he did this when the moon was big, and he came back in the morning, but that night there was no moon and he did not return.

I waited all that day for him until almost dusk and then I went out to look for him. I saw his tracks and followed them over the dunes and a hill to the lair where he had once lived. There I found him, lying in the back of the cave, alone. At first I thought that he had been hurt, yet there were no wounds on him. He touched my hand with his tongue, but only once and then he was quiet and scarcely breathed.

Since night had fallen and it was too dark for me to carry Rontu back, I stayed there. I sat beside him through the night and talked to him. At dawn I took him in my arms and left the cave. He was very light, as if something about him had already gone.

The sun was up as I went along the cliff. Gulls were crying in the sky. He raised his ears at the sound, and I put him down, thinking that he wished to bark at them as he always did. He raised his head and followed them with his eyes, but did not make a sound.

"Rontu," I said, "you have always liked to bark at the seagulls. Whole mornings and afternoons you have barked at them. Bark at them now for me."

But he did not look at them again. Slowly he walked to where I was standing and fell at my feet. I put my hand on his chest. I could feel his heart beating, but it beat only twice, very slowly, loud and hollow like the waves on the beach, and then no more.

"Rontu," I cried, "oh, Rontu!"

I buried him on the headland. I dug a hole in the crevice of the rock, digging for two days from dawn until the going down of the sun, and put him there with some sand flowers and a stick he liked to chase when I threw it, and covered him with pebbles of many colors that I gathered on the shore.

Chapter 26

That winter I did not go to the reef at all. I ate the things I had stored and left the house only to get water at the spring. It was a winter of strong winds and rains and wild seas that crashed against the cliffs, so I would not have gone out much even if Rontu had been there. During that time I made four snares from notched branches.

In the summer once, when I was on my way to the place where the sea elephants lived, I had seen a young dog that looked like Rontu. He was running with one of the packs of wild dogs, and though I caught only a glimpse of him, I was sure he was Rontu's son.

He was larger than the other dogs and had heavier fur and yellow eyes and he ran with a graceful stride like Rontu's. In the spring I planned to catch him with the snares I was making.

The wild dogs came to the headland often during the winter, now that Rontu was gone, and when the worst of the storms were over I set the snares outside the fence and baited them with fish. I caught several of the dogs the first time, but not the one with the yellow eyes, and since I was afraid to handle them, I was forced to let them free.

I made more snares and set these again, but while the wild dogs came close they would not touch the fish. I did catch a little red fox, which bit me when I took her out of the snare, yet she soon got over her wildness and would follow me around in the yard, begging for abalone. She was very much of a thief.

When I was away from the house, she always found some way to get into the food, no matter how well I hid it, so I had to let her go back to the ravine. Often, though, she would come at night and scratch at the fence for food.

I could not catch the young dog with a snare, and I was about to give up trying to when I thought of the toluache weed which we sometimes used to catch fish in the tide pools. It was not really a poison, but if you put it in the water the fish would turn over on their backs and float.

I remembered this weed and dug some where it grew on the far side of the island. I broke it up into small pieces which I dropped in the spring where the wild dogs drank. I waited all day and at dusk the pack came down to the spring. They drank their fill of the water, but nothing happened to them, or not much. They frisked around for a while, as I watched them from the brush, and trotted away.

I then remembered xuchal, which some of the men of our tribe used and is made from ground-up sea shells and wild tobacco. I made a big bowl of this, mixing it with water, and put it in the spring. I hid in the brush and waited. The dogs came at dusk. They sniffed the water and backed off and looked at each other, but at last began to drink. Soon afterward they began to walk around in circles. Suddenly they all lay down and went to sleep.

There were nine of them lying there by the spring. In the dim light it was hard to tell the one I wanted to take home, but finally I found him. He was snoring as if he had just eaten a big meal. I picked him up and hurried along the cliff, being frightened all the way that he would wake up before I reached the headland.

I pulled him through the opening under the fence

and tied him to it with a thong and left food beside him to eat and some fresh water. Before long he was on his feet, gnawing through the thong. He howled and ran about the yard while I cooked my supper. All night he howled, but at dawn when I went out of the house, he was asleep.

While he lay there by the fence sleeping, I thought of different names for him, trying first one and then another, saying them over to myself. At last, because he looked so much like his father, I called him Rontu-Aru, which means Son of Rontu.

In a short time he made friends with me. He was not so large as Rontu, but he had his father's thick coat and the same yellow eyes. Often when I watched him chasing gulls on the sandspit or on the reef barking at the otter, I forgot that he was not Rontu.

We had many happy times that summer, fishing and going to Tall Rock in our canoe, but more and more now I thought of Tutok and my sister Ulape. Sometimes I would hear their voices in the wind and often, when I was on the sea, in the waves that lapped softly against the canoe.

Chapter 27

After the fierce storms of winter came many days when the wind did not blow. The air was so heavy that it was hard to breathe and the sun so hot that the sea was like a sun itself, too bright to look at.

The last day of this weather I took the canoe from the cave and paddled around the reef to the sandspit. I did not take Rontu-Aru with me, for while he liked the cold he did not like heat. It was good that he did not come with me. The day was the hottest of all and the sea shimmered with red light. Over my eyes I wore shields made of wood with small slits in them to see through. No gulls were flying, the otter lay quiet in the kelp, and the little crabs were deep in their holes.

I pulled the canoe up on the beach, which was wet but steaming from the sun. Early every spring I took the canoe to the sandspit and spread fresh pitch in the cracks that needed it. I worked all this morning, stopping from time to time to cool off in the sea. As the sun climbed high I turned the canoe over and crawled under it and went to sleep in the shade.

I had not slept long when I was suddenly awakened by what I thought was thunder, but upon looking out from my shelter I saw that there were no clouds in the sky. Yet the rumbling sound kept on. It came from a distance, from the south and, as I listened, grew louder.

I jumped to my feet. The first thing that caught my gaze was the gleaming stretch of beach on the southern slope of the sandspit. Never in my life on the island had I seen the tide so low. Rocks and small reefs that I did not know were under the sea stood bare in the blinding light. It was like another place. I had gone to sleep and wakened on another island.

The air was suddenly tight around me. There was a faint sound as if some giant animal were sucking the air in and in through its teeth. The rumbling came closer out of an empty sky, filling my ears. Then beyond the gleam of the beach and the bare rocks and reefs, more than a league beyond them, I saw a great white crest moving down upon the island.

It seemed to move slowly between the sea and the sky, but it was the sea itself. I tore off the shields I wore over my eyes. In terror I ran along the sandspit. I ran and stumbled and got up and ran again. The sand shuddered under my feet as the first wave struck. Spray fell around me like rain. It was filled with pieces of kelp and small fish.

By following the curve of the sandspit I could reach the cove and the trail that led to the mesa, but there was no time for this. Water was already rushing around my knees, pulling from every direction. The cliff rose in front of me and though the rocks were slippery with sea moss I found a hold for a hand and then a foot. Thus, a step at a time, I dragged myself upward.

The crest of the wave passed under me and roared on toward Coral Cove.

For a time there was no sound. Then the sea began to seek its old place, running backward in long, foaming currents. Before it could do so another great wave moved out of the south. Perhaps it would be even bigger than the first one. I looked up. The cliff rose straight above me. I could climb no farther.

I stood facing the rock, with my feet on a narrow ledge and one hand thrust deep into a crack. Over my shoulder I could see the wave coming. It did not come fast, for the other wave was still running out. For a while I thought that it would not come at all because the two suddenly met beyond the sandspit. The first wave was trying to reach the sea and the second one was struggling toward the shore.

Like two giants they crashed against each other. They rose high in the air, bending first one way and then the other. There was a roar as if great spears were breaking in battle and in the red light of the sun the spray that flew around them looked like blood.

Slowly the second wave forced the first one backward, rolled slowly over it, and then as a victor drags the vanquished, moved in toward the island.

The wave struck the cliff. It sent long tongues streaming around me so that I could neither see nor hear. The tongues of water licked into all the crevices, dragged at my hand and at my bare feet gripping the ledge. They rose high above me along the face of the rock, up and up, and then spent themselves against the sky and fell back, hissing past me to join the water rushing on toward the cove.

Suddenly all around me was quiet. In the quiet I could hear my heart pounding and knew that my hand still had its hold on the rock and that I was alive.

Night came and though I was afraid to leave the cliff I knew that I could never stay there until morning, that I would go to sleep and fall. Neither could I find my way home, so I climbed down from the ledge and crouched at the foot of the cliff.

Dawn was windless and hot. The sandspit was strewn with hills of kelp. Dead fish and lobster and pink crabs lay everywhere, and two small whales were stranded against the rock walls of the cove. Far up the trail that led to the mesa I found things from the sea.

Rontu-Aru was waiting at the fence. When I crawled under it he jumped upon me and followed me around, never letting me out of his sight.

I was glad to be home on the high headland where the waves had not come. I had been gone only from one sun to the next, yet it was like many suns, like the time I had gone away in the canoe. Most of the day I slept, but I had many dreams and when I awoke everything around me was strange. The sea made no sounds on the shore. The gulls were quiet. The earth seemed to be holding its breath, as though it were waiting for something terrible to happen.

At dusk I was coming back from the spring with a basket of water on my shoulder, walking along the cliff with Rontu-Aru. Everywhere, the ocean was smooth and yellow and it lay against the island as if it were very tired. The gulls were still quiet, perched on their rocky nests.

Slowly the earth began to move. It moved away from my feet and for a moment I seemed to be standing in the air. Water tipped out of the basket and trickled over my face. Then the basket fell to the ground. Not knowing what I did, thinking foolishly that another wave was upon me, I began to run. But it *was* a wave, a wave of earth, and it rippled under me along the cliff.

As I ran another wave overtook me. Looking back I saw many of them coming out of the south like waves in the sea. The next thing I remember I was lying on the ground and Rontu-Aru was beside me and we were both trying to get to our feet. Then we were running again toward the headland, toward a house that kept moving off into the distance.

The opening under the fence had caved in and I had to pull the rocks away before we could crawl through. Night came, but the earth still rose and fell like a great animal breathing. I could hear rocks tumbling from the cliff, falling down into the sea.

All night as we lay there in the house the earth trembled and rocks fell, yet not the big one on the headland, which would have fallen if those who make the world shake had really been angry with us.

In the morning the earth was quiet once more and a fresh wind that smelled of kelp blew out of the northern sea.

Chapter 28

The earthquake did little damage. Even the spring, which failed to flow for several days, started up again and flowed more than ever. But the great waves had cost me all the food and weapons which were stored in the cave, as well as the canoe I had been working on and those hidden under the south cliffs.

The canoes were the biggest loss. To find enough wood to make another would have taken me all the spring and summer. I therefore set out on the first fair morning to search for whatever wreckage the waves had washed ashore.

Among the rocks near the south cliffs I found a part of one canoe, buried in sand and twisted kelp. I worked all morning to dig it free and then, having scraped it clean, could not decide what to do. I could cut the sinews and carry the planks up the cliff two at a time on my back and across the dunes to Coral Cove, which meant many days. Or I could build the canoe here on the rocks and take the chance that another storm would wash it away before I was finished.

I finally did neither of these things. Choosing a day when the sea was calm, I floated what was left of the canoe and, pushing it in front of me, made my way past the sandspit and into the cove. There I took the wreckage apart and moved the planks up the trail, beyond the place where the great waves had reached.

I found the remains of my other canoe. It had been washed far back in the cave and I could not get it out, so I went back to the south cliffs and hunted among the piles of kelp until I had enough pieces of wood, counting what I already had, to begin the building of another.

It was late in the spring now. The weather was still unsettled, with light rain falling most of the days, but I started the new canoe anyway, for I needed it to gather shellfish. No longer did I think of the Aleuts, as I have said, yet without a canoe to go where I wanted, I felt uneasy.

The planks were all about the same size, the length of my arm, but they came from different canoes and were therefore hard to fit together. The holes were ready, however, which saved me much labor and time. Another help was that the great waves had washed ashore long strings of black pitch, which was often difficult to find on the island and which I needed.

When I had sorted out the planks and shaped them, the work went fast, so that by late spring I was ready to finish the seams. It was on a windy morning that I made a fire to soften the pitch. The wind was cold and it took a long time to get the fire going. To hasten it I went down to the beach for dry seaweed.

I had started back with my arms filled when I turned to look at the sky, thinking from the feel of the wind that a storm might be close. Off to the north the skies were clear, but in the east from whence storms sometimes came at this season, stood banks of gray clouds, one on top of the other.

At this moment, in the deep shadows cast by the clouds, I saw something else. Forgetting that I was carrying a load of seaweed, I threw up my arms. The seaweed fell to the ground.

A sail, a ship, was there on the sea, halfway

between the horizon and the shore!

By the time I had reached the headland it was much closer, moving quickly on the strong wind. I could see that it did not have the red, beaked prow of the Aleuts. Nor did it look like the white men's ship, which I clearly remembered.

Why had it come to the Island of the Blue Dolphins?

I crouched on the headland and wondered, my heart beating fast, if the men who sailed it had come to catch otter. If they were hunters, I must hide before they saw me. They would soon find my fire and the canoe I was making, yet I could go to the cave and probably be safe from them. But if they had been sent by my people to take me away, then I should not hide.

The ship moved slowly between the black rocks and into Coral Cove. I could see the men now and they were not Aleuts.

They lowered a canoe and two of the men paddled toward the beach. The wind had begun to blow hard and the men had trouble landing. Finally one of them stayed behind in the canoe, and the other, the man without a beard, jumped into the water and came along the beach and up the trail.

I could not see him, but after a while I heard a shout, then another, and I knew that he had found my fire and the canoe. The man he had left in the cove did not answer, nor did the men in the ship, so I was sure that he was calling to me.

I crawled down from the rock and went to the house. Since my shoulders were bare, I put on my otter cape. I took my cormorant skirt and the abalone box in which I kept my necklace and earrings. With Rontu-Aru I then went along the trail that led to Coral Cove.

I came to the mound where my ancestors had sometimes camped in the summer. I thought of them and of the happy times spent in my house on the headland, of my canoe lying unfinished beside the trail. I thought of many things, but stronger was the wish to be where people lived, to hear their voices and their laughter.

I left the mound and the green grass growing on it among the white shells. I could no longer hear the man calling, so I began to run. When I came to the place where the two trails met, where I had built my fire, I found the footsteps the man had left.

I followed them down to the cove. The canoe had gone back to the ship. The wind was screaming now and mist blew in across the harbor and waves began to pile up on the shore. I raised my hand and shouted. I shouted over and over, but the wind carried my voice away. I ran down the beach and waded into the water. The men did not see me.

Rain started to fall and the wind drove it against my face. I waded farther out through the waves, raising my arms to the ship. Slowly it moved away in the mist. It went toward the south. I stood there until it was out of sight.

Chapter 29

After two more springs had gone, on a morning of white clouds and calm seas, the ship came back. At dawn I saw it from the headland far out on the horizon. When the sun was overhead it lay anchored in Coral Cove.

Until the sun went down I watched from the headland while the men made a camp on the shore and built a fire. Then I went to my house. All night I did not sleep, thinking of the man who once had called to me.

I had thought of his voice for a long time, since the night of the storm when the ship had sailed away. Every day during those two springs and two summers I had gone to the headland and watched, always at dawn and again at dusk.

In the morning I smelled smoke from their fire. I went down to the ravine and bathed in the spring and put on my otter cape and my cormorant skirt. I put on the necklace of black stones and the black earrings. With blue clay I made the mark of our tribe across my nose.

Then I did something that made me smile at myself. I did what my older sister Ulape had done when she left the Island of the Blue Dolphins. Below the mark of our tribe I carefully made the sign which meant that I was still unmarried. I was no longer a girl, yet I made it anyway, using the blue clay and some white clay for the dots.

I went back to the house then and built a fire and

cooked food for Rontu-Aru and me. I was not hungry and he ate my food and his too.

"We are going away," I said to him, "away from our island."

But he only put his head to one side, as his father often had done, and when I said no more, he trotted out to a sunny place and lay down and fell asleep.

Now that the white men had come back, I could not think of what I would do when I went across the sea, or make a picture in my mind of the white men and what they did there, or see my people who had been gone so long. Nor, thinking of the past, of the many summers and winters and springs that had gone, could I see each of them. They were all one, a tight feeling in my breast and nothing more.

The morning was full of sun. The wind smelled of the sea and the things that lived in it. I saw the men long before they saw the house on the headland, far off on the dunes to the south. There were three of them, two tall men and one who was short and wore a long gray robe. They left the dunes and came along the cliff, and then seeing the smoke from the fire which I kept burning, they followed it, and at last reached my house.

I crawled under the fence and stood facing them. The man in the gray robe had a string of beads around his neck and at the end of it was an ornament of polished wood. He raised his hand and made a motion toward me which was the shape of the ornament he wore. Then one of the two men who stood behind him spoke to me. His words made the strangest sounds I have ever heard. At first I wanted to laugh, but I bit my tongue.

I shook my head and smiled at him. He spoke again, slowly this time, and though his words sounded the same as before and meant nothing to me, they now seemed sweet. They were the sound of a human voice. There is no sound like this in all the world.

The man lifted his hand and pointed toward the cove and made a picture in the air of what could have been a ship.

To this I nodded and myself pointed to the three baskets I had placed by the fire, making a gesture of taking them with me to the ship. Also the cage in which I had put two young birds.

There were many gestures before we left, though the two men spoke among themselves. They liked my necklace, the cape, and the cormorant skirt that shone in the sun. But when we got to the beach, where their camp was, the first thing the man who spoke the most did was tell the other men to make me a dress.

I knew this was what he said because one of them stood in front of me and held up a string from my neck to my feet and across my shoulders.

The dress was blue. It was made of two trousers, just like those the white men were wearing. The trousers were cut up into pieces and then one of the men sat down on a rock and put them together again with white string. He had a long nose, which looked like the needle he used. He sat all afternoon on the rock and the needle went back and forth, in and out, flashing in the sun.

From time to time he would hold up the dress and nod his head as if he were pleased. I nodded as if I were pleased, too, but I was not. I wanted to wear my cormorant skirt and my otter cape, which were much more beautiful than the thing he was making.

The dress reached from my throat to my feet and I

did not like it, either the color of it or the way it scratched. It was also hot. But I smiled and put my cormorant skirt away in one of the baskets to wear when I got across the sea, sometime when the men were not around.

The ship stayed in Coral Cove nine days. It had come for otter, but the otter had gone. Some must have been left, after all, who remembered the Aleuts, for on that morning there were none to be seen.

I knew where they had gone. They had gone to Tall Rock, but when the men showed me the weapons they had brought to kill the otter, I shook my head and acted as though I did not understand. They pointed to my otter cape, but I still shook my head.

I asked them then about the ship that had taken my people away many years before, making the signs of the ship and pointing to the east, but they did not understand. Not until I came to Mission Santa Barbara and met Father Gonzales did I learn from him that this ship had sunk in a great storm soon after it reached his country and that on the whole ocean thereabouts there was no other. For this reason, the white men had not come back for me.

On the tenth day we sailed. It was a morning of blue skies and no wind. We went straight toward the sun.

For a long time I stood and looked back at the Island of the Blue Dolphins. The last thing I saw of it was the high headland. I thought of Rontu lying there beneath the stones of many colors, and of Won-a-nee, wherever she was, and the little red fox that would scratch in vain at my fence, and my canoe hidden in the cave, and of all the happy days.

Dolphins rose out of the sea and swam before the ship. They swam for many leagues in the morning through the bright water, weaving their foamy patterns. The little birds were chirping in their cage and Rontu-Aru sat beside me.

Author's Note

The island called in this book the Island of the Blue Dolphins was first settled by Indians in about 2000 B.C., but it was not discovered by white men until 1602.

In that year the Spanish explorer Sebastián Vizcaíno set out from Mexico in search of a port where treasure galleons from the Philippines could find shelter in case of distress. Sailing north along the California coast, he sighted the island, sent a small boat ashore and named it La Isla de San Nicolas, in honor of the patron saint of sailors, travelers, and merchants.

As the centuries passed, California changed from Spanish to Mexican hands, the Americans arrived, but only occasional hunters visited the island. Its Indian inhabitants remained in isolation.

The girl Robinson Crusoe whose story I have attempted to re-create actually lived alone upon this island from 1835 to 1853, and is known to history as The Lost Woman of San Nicolas.

The facts about her are few. From the reports of Captain Hubbard, whose schooner carried away the Indians of Ghalas-at, we know that the girl did jump into the sea, despite efforts to restrain her. From records left by Captain Nidever we know that he found her eighteen years later, alone with a dog in a crude house on the headland, dressed in a skirt of cormorant feathers. Father Gonzales of Santa Barbara Mission, who befriended her after her rescue, learned that her brother had been killed by wild dogs. He learned little else, for she spoke to him only in signs; neither he nor the many Indians at the mission could understand her strange language. The Indians of Ghalas-at had long since disappeared.

The Lost Woman of San Nicolas is buried on a hill near the Santa Barbara Mission. Her skirt of green cormorant feathers was sent to Rome.

Outermost of the eight Channel Islands, San Nicolas is about seventy-five miles southwest of Los Angeles. For years historians thought that it had been settled some six centuries ago, but recent carbon-14 tests of excavations on the island show that Indians came here from the north long before the Christian era. Their images of the creatures of the land, sea, and air, similar to those found on the shores of Alaska and carved with extraordinary skill, may be seen at the Southwest Museum in Los Angeles.

The future of San Nicolas is not clear. It is now a secret base of the United States Navy, but scientists predict that because of the pounding waves and furious winds it will one day be swept back into the sea.

In the writing of the *Island of the Blue Dolphins,* I am deeply indebted to Maude and Delos Lovelace, to Bernice Eastman Johnson of the Southwest Museum, and to Fletcher Carr, formerly curator of the San Diego Museum of Man.

Related Readings

CONTENTS

The Dolphin Walking Stick

by Georgiana Valoyce-Sanchez

Karana, the heroine of Island of the
Blue Dolphins, *belonged to the Chumash*
(choo' măsh) *people who once lived on the
Channel Islands off the coast of southern
California. The writer of the following
poem is a modern-day Chumash woman.
In the poem, her father describes how
he chose the dolphin as his personal
symbol. Then he retells an ancient
legend explaining why the Chumash
feel a kinship to dolphins.*

He says
sure you look for your Spirit
symbol   your totem
only it's more a waiting
5   watching
for its coming

You listen
You listen for the way it
feels   deep inside

10   Sometimes something comes
that feels   almost
right
the way that swordfish
kept cropping up with
15   its long nose

but no
and so   you wait
knowing it is getting
closer   knowing
20   it is coming

And when that dolphin
jumped out of the water
its silver blue sides all shiny
and glistening with rainbows
25   against the white cloud sky
and the ocean so big
and deep
it went on
forever
30   I knew it had come

My father rests his hand upon
the dolphin's back
the dolphin's gaze serene
above the rainbow band
35   wrapped around the walking stick

He leans upon his brother friend
and walks across the room

   As he walks
strings of seashells clack softly
40   like when ocean waves tumble
rocks and shells and
the gentle clacking song
follows each wave

as it pulls back into
45   the sea

The sea

So long ago
The Channel Islands filled
with Chumash People like
colonies of sea lions
along the shore so many
people
it was time for some to
make the move
across the ocean to
the mainland

Kakunupmawa the sun
the Great Mystery
according to men's ideas
said
don't worry
I will make you a bridge
the rainbow
will be your bridge only
don't look down
or you will fall
Have Faith
So the chosen ones began
the long walk across
the rainbow
they kept their eye straight
toward where the mainland was
and all around them
was the ocean sparkling
like a million scattered crystals
so blue-green and singing
lovely and cool
some looked down

and fell
80 into the deep
    to become
    the dolphins
    they too
    the People

85 My father turns to look at me

    Someone told me that story
    long before I ever heard it
    It's those old ones
    he says pointing up to the ceiling
90 as if it were sky

    They sent the dolphin to me

    I always loved the sea

from The World of the Sea Otter

by Stefani Paine

Sea otters are very important in Island of
the Blue Dolphins. *It is to hunt sea otters
that the deadly Aleuts come to Karana's
island. Later, when Karana is lonely, she
makes a pet of the young otter Mon-a-nee
and is amused by watching it feed. This
selection by a marine biologist describes in
fascinating detail how sea otters collect
and eat their food.*

Somewhere in the distance, you hear a series of
sharp, rapid clicks. Moving in on the scene, you spot
a sea otter floating on its back, a clam held firmly
between two flat paws, and a blur of short arms
working together as the sea otter bangs the clam on
its chest, as if driving a spike with both arms.
Coming closer, you see a good-sized rock cradled in
the animal's chest fur. The sea otter uses it like an
anvil, repeatedly banging the clam on it. At last the
banging stops, and after a rapid roll in the water, the
otter is eating the clam. Quickly, mouth, teeth and
paws are working together. The otter tosses pieces of
shell aside as its strong, white teeth scrape off the
fleshy bits. There is more chewing, followed by
another quick roll, and the sea otter reappears with
another clam, like a magician pulling a coin from the
air. The entire process is repeated until four or five
good-size clams have been cracked open and

consumed. Another roll and the rock disappears. Now the sea otter will groom and rest.

Returning three or four hours later when the sea otter is ready to eat again, you might find it collecting heavy-shelled snails, spidery crabs, thousand-spined sea urchins, Chinese hat limpets, deep blue mussels, a black leathery chiton, a rock scallop, a flatfish or a ragged tube worm. You might see it chew the arm off an orange sea star or pull a reluctant hermit crab from its shell.

The sea otter is an efficient hunter and will collect and eat just about any fish or invertebrate animal it can find. Other true marine mammals, including whales, dolphins, seals and sea lions, have the advantage of speed and range. They can chase and catch fast-moving fish, which they swallow underwater. Although the sea otter is too slow for most fish, except the sluggish bottom fish species, it has a great advantage in being able to use its forepaws. In contrast, seals and dolphins can eat only what they can catch with their jaws alone. And unless they bite off a chunk of something, they are limited to what they can swallow whole. These animals also catch and swallow underwater, "on the fly." The sea otter always eats at the surface, spreading its bounty on its chest, as if it were a lunch counter.

The sea otter plays and rests on the sea's surface, but it hunts on the sea floor. In readiness for a dive, the otter sucks in a full breath of air and rolls forward in one strong and graceful turn. Now an invisible clock begins to tick. Seconds march by as the otter holds its forepaws across its chest and propels itself downward with powerful undulations of its body, hind flippers held together and spread in a dolphin-like pose. The clock continues to tick. Now on the sea bottom, the otter navigates with great flexibility by alternate sweeps of its hind flippers and overhand pulls with its forearms. As the otter spots urchins, crabs or other edibles, it swiftly tucks them into loose skin folds under each arm, which act like built-in shopping bags. Tick, tick—time is almost out as the otter runs out of air. The otter has worked hard, swimming down perhaps 18 or 20 meters (60 or 66 feet), moved quickly, searched for and collected food, making the most of precious seconds before it is forced to the surface to breathe. If the trip had not been successful, the otter would dive again and again in successive trips of thirty, sixty or ninety seconds.

On another trip, it might use its sensitive whiskers to locate small crabs or snails hidden in the dense seaweed mats, or reach into crevices and pat under boulders with equally sensitive forepaws, feeling for low-profile limpets or chitons hidden from view. The sea otter's paws are a little like flat mitts. They do not look particularly agile or manipulative, but they are. Combined with short, semi-retractable claws, the paws are surprisingly strong and agile. Otters will use both paws together to rub, roll, twist and pull with great strength and dexterity. Playing with the young sea otters that had been hand-reared after their mothers had died in the *Exxon Valdez* oil spill, I learned just how mobile and efficient these paws could be. The otters loved to nuzzle and feel everything. They could remove rings from fingers in an instant and steal buttons, belts and objects in pockets with the slick ease of a pickpocket. A tug of war over a set of keys demonstrated the sea otter's surprising strength for its size.

This great dexterity is of enormous advantage when searching out and collecting smaller food items. Sea otters can comb kelp fronds in search of kelp crabs and snails or, underwater, search in the complicated kelp's holdfast for the many creatures that seek refuge there.

The sea otter's skill at collecting abalone has not only angered commercial abalone divers but also challenged biologists trying to determine how this small animal can dislodge the huge, flat snails. Abalone have two avenues of defense: a large, heavy shell and the power to clamp down with great force when disturbed. It is estimated that an abalone may exert a suction equal to 4,000 times its own weight. Abalone divers use a flat iron bar as a crowbar to dislodge the abalone, which can be as much as 15 to 25 centimeters (6 to 10 inches) across and contain up to a kilogram (a couple of pounds) of body meat. Underwater observations reveal that the sea otter uses a stone about the size of a large softball to dislodge the abalone. Holding the stone in both paws, the sea otter uses it to hammer the side of the abalone shell at the rate of 45 blows in 15 seconds. Abalone are big, thick-shelled and tough. Sea otters are persistent, determined and willful. Although it may take one, two or even three episodes of abalone bashing, eventually the sea otter emerges with its prize.

Sea otters are also great clam diggers, successfully collecting a variety of species, from the prized pismo clam to smaller sand clams and razor clams. Clams do not sit on the sand waiting to be picked up by the sea otter any more than they sit on the sand waiting to be picked up by recreational diggers. Clams must be dug. Since the clams live embedded in the sand 10 to 50 centimeters (4 to 20 inches) below the surface, the sea otter begins by digging a trench. Working head down and using its forepaws to dig, much like a dog digs in the sand, the sea otter excavates a trench in a series of short, energetic digging sessions of about half a minute each. Subsequent dives enlarge the trench, as the sea otter digs into the side of the trench searching for clams. In the end, the trench may be 0.5 meter (1 1/2 feet) deep and wide and 1.5 meters (5 feet) long. Since the largest clams are generally the deepest, this deep digging makes sense. For example, the butter clam, *Saxidomus giganteus,* lives as deep as 50 centimeters (20 inches).

The sea otter's eagerness to explore anything and everything within its environment as a source of food is somewhat unusual in an adult animal. This characteristic has no doubt contributed to its ability to thrive over such an extensive geographical range. The food species eaten in the Aleutians, for example, are not the same as those eaten in California. This constant search and determination to exploit potential food sources is well illustrated by an otter observed in Monterey Bay that had made the connection between discarded soft drink cans and small octopuses. Young octopuses will seek shelter in any crevice offering a small entrance and protection from predators. Since octopuses are soft-bodied except for their hard, parrot-like beak, they can squeeze themselves through the smallest openings, the size of which is determined by the size of their beaks. In the same way that a large, flaccid, water-filled balloon could be worked through a very small hole, an octopus can gain entry through very small openings. It is not surprising that small octopuses in Monterey Bay have taken up residence in discarded cans.

Biologists watching sea otters in Monterey Bay in

the 1970s saw a sea otter bite open a pop can. Within the next 15 minutes, seven more cans were retrieved, five of which contained octopuses. It took the otter an average of thirty seconds to open each can. Divers checking the area later discovered 22 cans. Eight had already been opened, and half of the remaining cans contained octopuses of up to 35 centimeters (14 inches) from arm to arm. Doubtless the sea otter would be back again for canned octopus.

Incisors on both upper and lower jaws are used to wedge open shells, bite through urchin tests and scrape out shells. Large, flat molars grind and chew. When eating a large crab, for example, the otter holds the crab on its chest, ripping the legs off and chewing them one at a time. Then, holding the carapace, or top shell, in both paws, the otter uses its teeth to open the shell. The otter holds the crab shell like a large bowl against its mouth as it scrapes and licks out any remaining edible parts.

The same system is used for large urchins and abalone. Like any other part of an otter's foraging and feeding behavior, the activity is brisk, efficient and energetic. For a not-so-large animal, a sea otter can put away a remarkable amount of seafood in one meal. For example, one otter ate 24 pismo clams (average 10 to 13 centimeters, or 4 to 5 inches) and 2 spiny mole crabs in 2 hours and 15 minutes. Another ate 14 large pismo clams and 37 spiny mole crabs in 4 hours.

Although the sea otter grooms on and off all day, it does so most vigorously after a bout of diving and eating. The repeated rhythm of dive-collect-eat, dive-collect-eat, has lasted an hour or more. Now it is time for the otter to wash up, to scrub, lick and rinse every hair of its magnificent coat. Each bit of oil and debris will be washed away, as every centimeter of fur on every part of the otter's body is attacked with the same meticulous vigor. It is also time to restore the fur's depleted air layer. With each foraging dive, the sea otter loses more air from its fur. As it plunges deeper and deeper, air escapes in a mist of fine bubbles that follows the diving otter like a cloud of underwater dust. Just as any air-filled container released underwater rockets to the surface, so the layer of air trapped in the sea otter's fine underfur squeezes out between the guard hairs as the otter dives deeper, the water pressure increases, and the air fights to escape.

Air pressed out of the otter's fur will not automatically be replaced by a simple shrug and a shake. It must be painstakingly restored as the sea otter alternately rubs and lifts handfuls of fur to its mouth, first drying the fur and then blowing warm air back into it. The principle is the same as that of the hair dryer used by hairdressers to give temporary lift and fullness to a human head of hair. Eventually the reduced air blanket is brought back to the otter's satisfaction and it is time to rest.

The well-fed, well-groomed otter raises its large, furred hind flippers out of the water and arranges them one over the other across its abdomen. With head resting forward on its chest, the otter covers its eyes with its forepaws, hooks them behind its head as if to support its neck or simply holds its arms straight up, as if it were a surgeon waiting to receive sterile gloves. Now it closes its eyes and sleeps, absolutely still except for the slow sculling of its tail.

The Ice-Hearts

by Joseph Bruchac

In the following story, an Iroquois village in the American Northeast is attacked by invaders. Like Karana, the narrator faces a difficult choice when he at last captures the enemies who have killed two of his people.

It was the Moon of Long Nights when the Ice-Hearts came to us. They came down the long river which flows north to shores where the water is filled with salt and goes on without ending. Along the northern bank of that river they had walked and then, at a place where winter closed the lips of the stream, they crossed.

Ice was frozen to their faces, frozen in the hair that covered their faces. Their clothing was grey and hard, the color of flint. They carried long knives and big axes shiny as ice. And their hearts, it seemed, were made of ice, too, for they came down on our peaceful village and killed, the coldness of ice in their sky-colored eyes. They killed and stole food and then vanished back into the storm which seemed to have given them birth.

They were hard fighters, but not all of them got away. Two of them we caught among the small trees. One was tangled in some vines and the other stood by him, cutting him free. We circled them. They turned slowly from side to side as we circled. We could see then that it was not their skin which was hard as flint, so hard our arrows broke when they struck, but some kind of armor they were wearing. We knew of armor, for some of us wore armor when we fought, an armor made of hard pieces of wood. We moved closer . . . and one of them raised his axe up quickly, as if he meant to throw it. That was when Big Duck threw himself to the ground. He dropped just like a duck hit by an arrow and as he hit the ground he farted.

That was so funny that we all laughed. Eagle Circling, Eats Like A Bear, and even Big Duck himself as he lay there. Maybe those ice-hearted men were going to kill some of us, maybe we were going to kill them, but this was funny. And I, Fox Looking Around, I laughed the hardest, I think. But I kept my eye on the Ice-Hearts as I laughed. I was not ready to die laughing. But they were laughing, too! When Death has a hand on your shoulder you do strange things. Just as we laughed, they laughed, a laughter which took away the grimness and anger from their eyes. That was when we saw how young they were. And as they laughed we came up to them and took away their long knives and axes.

Two people had died when the Ice-Hearts came. One was an old man sleeping by the door of the longhouse. His nickname was Goes In The Corner because he always hated to go outside when winter came. Even though his wife was very stern with him, the part of the longhouse where they lived sometimes smelled of urine. The leader of the Ice-Hearts stuck his long knife right through the old man's stomach when he stood as they forced their way in through the door. Old Goes In The Corner shouted once and then fell, half in and half out the door. People woke up fast then. It seemed as if a Whirlwind had forced its way into the longhouse. Some people tried to get as far away from that door as they could. Others grabbed weapons and formed a half circle to face the invaders. Someone threw dry wood on the central fire and it blazed up, showing us the tall figures of strange men who looked like no people we had ever seen before. More of them forced their way in, standing shoulder to shoulder, until there were at least as many of them as there were of our fighting men facing them, and there were twenty of us standing between them and our old people, our children, and our women.

The one who stood in front of the others made a noise. It may have been words, but it was no language we had heard before. It was hard to believe a human being could make such sounds. Those sounds made some of our people wonder if these strange men were from the world of spirits. As soon as the one in front stopped growling, though, Casts Light stepped forward.

Casts Light was a brave man. His dreams in the past had showed him how to do good things and he had a reputation as a healer. He advanced on the Ice-Hearts, holding an Eagle feather in front of him as if it were a burning branch. He shook it at the One In Front and was about to say something, but his words never left his mouth. There was a sudden flash as the One In Front's blade swept through the air. The Eagle feather fell to the ground in two pieces and Casts Light fell beside it, his head almost cut from his body. It was an evil deed and we waited no longer. Whether men or spirits, we had to drive them out. The One In Front was grabbing now at the pieces of meat drying above the fire. We let fly with our weapons.

Most of our arrows and spears bounced off their hard bodies, but the Ice-Hearts began making a great noise and moved back towards the door. Their strange eyes flashed in the firelight and they swung their weapons at us, but we stayed back, picking up our arrows as they bounced off and firing again. Now the women were shouting out war songs. "Do not let these People of Ice kill our children," they cried, and it urged us on. Then an arrow hurt the One In Front. Whether by luck or good aim, it went into one of the few places which was not armored on his body—it struck him in the eye. His hands went up to his face and he fell backwards. The others grabbed him and dragged him with them. They were out the door now, going back along the tracks Grandmother Moon showed us they had made in the deep soft snow as they came upon our longhouse. Another of the Ice-Hearts fell, a spear piercing his neck. He, too, was carried off by the others. They moved quickly, those big men. Most of us were not quick to follow.

That was when I called my three friends aside. They had come with me once when we went to raid against the People Who Live Where The Dawn Begins. I held up my snowshoes and made a half circle motion over the hill. They understood. If we went that way we might be able to cut off some of the Ice-Hearts from the others. And so it happened.

When we came back to the longhouse everyone, the living and the dead, was there. There was a smell in the air like that of a slaughtered deer and there was dark blood frozen in the snow at the door. Sounds of mourning filled the air. But as we pushed the two big men ahead of us, the sounds turned into shouts of wonder. We were carrying the weapons of the Ice-Hearts, and they had been so well armed that each of us had something. I carried a big shield which was cold to the touch as stone. Eats Like A Bear had one of the long knives and so did Eagle Circling. Sore Eyes had chosen an axe, the best choice of all of us. He would use that axe for many years clearing space for cornfields and cutting poles for lodges. Big Duck, who had defeated them, carried two smaller knives which he juggled from hand to hand. He was trying to look serious and strong, but the laughter kept creeping back into his eyes.

The women came close. Some of them made remarks about the size of the men and jabbed sticks at them. They were making jokes, but they were angry. Two women no longer had husbands and there were children without a father now. If we had handed the Ice-Hearts over to the women then, they would have killed them. Instead, we took our captives to the fire in the center. There we removed the armor from them. Without their heavy coats the men were still big, but they were thin. Their ribs showed and the bones of their shoulders stuck out like the knobs of war clubs. That was why they attacked us then? For food because they were starving?

"But there is plenty of game around here," said Pretty Eyes, the wife of Eagle Circling.

"Maybe they only know how to fight and not how to hunt," I suggested. Some of the people looked at me as if they thought I was crazy, but later on they would see I was right. The weapons the Ice-Hearts carried were not for hunting game animals. The place they came from must have been strange indeed if it bred men who knew only how to kill other human beings and not how to hunt to keep themselves and their families alive.

We tied the hands of the two big men and made them sit down near the fire. Near them were the bodies of the two their people killed. Outside, the Sun, our Elder Brother, was rising. He must have been disappointed, for he is the one who loves fighting and war the best and it all had happened while our Grandmother, the moon, was in the sky. To us, though, it was neither day nor night now. Something had happened which never had happened before. It was the time to talk and listen to wise voices.

Each person who wished to speak was given a chance. Many wished to kill the men right away.

"We have been calling these creatures Ice-Hearts," said a man named Wood Tick, "because they are like the monsters in the old stories. Let us see if their hearts really are made of ice. If we cut them out, then we can tell."

"Let us see how brave they are," said a woman named Swaying Reeds. "Let us see if they know any Death Songs."

I, too, had my chance to speak. "These people," I said, "they belong to me and my friends, I think. We caught them. We give them, though, to everyone here. All of you can decide what to do with them. I am not very wise and I cannot say what should be done. If we keep them, though, they may be good workers. Many people here have relatives who were adopted in the past. Now they are part of us. Two of our people are dead. Now we have two captives. Maybe someone will take them in. Maybe they can learn to talk like real human beings and tell us about the place they came from. I have said enough. That is all I have to say."

So we continued to talk. The time came to eat and we untied the hands of the two men. They were surprised, but they ate with us, ate like men who are hungry but also grateful to be fed. Then we talked further. The Sun was going down when everyone had spoken. I had been pleased to hear words like my own, though spoken better and clearer—for the waters of age run deeper and hold more fish than the swift streams of youth. The Old Men Who Wear The Horns of Office, those who spoke for us at the meetings of the Great League, they had seen things as I saw them. That was good. They had been listening, as they always do, to the Clan Mothers, those women whose words are sometimes not heard in council, but who point the way to any decision.

In the end, the two men were adopted. We made this clear to them by signs which they understood.

The younger-looking one, whose face was very thin with a big beak of a nose under a thatch of hair the color of fire was adopted by the widow of old Goes In The Corner.

"He will be my son," she said. "I'm going to call him Woodpecker."

The other was adopted by the family of Casts Light. There were grim scars on his chest and thighs which showed he had been a warrior for some time. The hair on his head was the color of autumn grass, but he was hairy all over his body and especially on his chest and those hairs were very black. Bear Chest is what we called him. That was appropriate in more ways than we knew. The Bear Clan adopted him and the Bear Clan has always been known for its healers. It turned out that Bear Chest knew how to set broken limbs and knew other ways of healing which helped many. Casts Light's uncle taught him other things about medicine and the fame of Bear Chest as a doctor spread among our people as years passed.

They never left us. They grew fat from our food and married good women who gave us many children. At first they called us "Sgah-lay-leens," a word from their old language. But as they learned our words, the past and their old way of talking fell away from them as leaves fall from the maples during the Moon of Falling Leaves and with spring the green buds of real human speech opened from their mouths.

We saw no more of their people. Stories came to us over the years. The People of the Dawn passed on tales of big men like our Ice-Hearts. They came in canoes larger than a lodge and fought the way our Ice-Hearts fought. But all of them were wiped out and no more boats came. They were like the storms which blow in sometimes from the big salt water. Those storms are strong at first, but they falter and die after moving inland. Storms come and go, but the Earth stays.

I, Fox Looking Around, am a very old man. Woodpecker and Bear Chest have been dead for many seasons and some of you are their children. Your skins are pale, perhaps, and some of you have eyes the color of the sky. But you are real human beings, just as your fathers became real human beings after we adopted them. Your children will look more like us still. That is the way it has always been. But I do not think, as do all the rest of our people, that the story of the Ice-Hearts is over. True, we learned that the Ice-Hearts are men. We learned that laughter is a great weapon, a defense which can melt a cold heart. But I believe that one day more of those people of the storm, those people who know how to kill other human beings but do not know how to grow crops or hunt, will come to this place where we live. There may be more of them then and they may have strange ideas of keeping the land for themselves the way you might keep a favorite ball or a pair of moccasins.

Listen, for this is the way Woodpecker explained it to me after he had lived with us for many seasons.

"Fox," he said, "you are my brother and I never had a brother before. You are closer to me now than Eric . . . Bear Chest, for he is a man with a good heart but he does not think very much. So I want to tell you something, something you must promise to pass on to our children. I tell you this for you understand better than the others who just nod and then look away when I tell them. We came to this place to take land. We came from a place where there was not land enough for our people. Instead, this land took us. It has not ended, though. Others like my people will come someday. But I have thought and thought hard and this is what I think. I think that more people will die next time. You will have to fight and keep on fighting for a long time. But this land of yours is strong, Fox Looking Around. It is strong and you know that. If you stay close to this land, if you do not give it up, it will win again. Tell that to our children."

And, all of my life, that is what I have done. This is where my story ends.

Courage

by Dudley Randall

This speaker sees a new side of courage.

There are degrees of courage.
One man is not afraid to die.
A second is not afraid to kill.
A third is not afraid to be merciful.

from The Girl with the White Flag

by Tomiko Higa

*This excerpt is from the true story of
another young girl abandoned and left to
survive on her own. In April 1945, during
the last stages of World War II, the U.S.
Army attacked Japanese forces on the
island of Okinawa. As the fighting
advanced toward their home, 7-year-old
Tomiko was forced to flee south with her
older sisters Yoshiko and Hatsuko, and her
beloved 9-year-old brother Nini. Days later,
when they reached Komesu beach, they
dug shallow holes to sleep in while shells
and machine gun bullets rained around
them. The girls woke to find that Nini had
been killed by a stray bullet. They buried
him in the sand before being driven off
by soldiers.*

Fleeing Alone

Leaving our hearts there, we walked away from
Komesu beach, casting many a backward glance at
the mound of sand where we had buried Nini.
Komesu, which I later located on the map, is at the
southernmost tip of the main island of Okinawa. In
our flight, we had covered about nine miles in a
direct line from home.

As far as Komesu, Nini had held my hand the
whole way, and now I clutched a corner of Hatsuko's

garment as I walked. The road was crowded with people who had been driven away from Komesu beach, and I hung on to Hatsuko's clothes very tightly, almost running to keep up, for fear of becoming separated from my sisters.

Some time later, I happened to look up at Hatsuko, whose face was only barely visible in the starlight. To my horror, the face was not Hatsuko's. Nor was it Yoshiko's. It was that of a woman I had never seen before. The woman whose garment I had been clutching all this time was a total stranger. I did not know how it could have happened.

I let go my hand and started running hither and yon, looking at the face of this young woman and that, but could find neither Hatsuko nor Yoshiko anywhere.

I was all alone.

Thinking I would find them soon, I spent the night in a grassy spot away from the road, for sleep had overcome my determination to find my sisters.

Searching for them was impossible in the daytime, however, as enemy action was so severe that all one could do was hide in a cave until nightfall. Moreover, I had nothing with me at all—nothing to eat and no change of clothes—and I felt terribly lonely and frightened.

I could not wait for night to fall, and left my place of hiding. I ran from cave to cave calling out "Sister! Sister!" only to be shooed away by the cave's denizens the way you would shoo away an unwanted cat or dog.

Finally, exhausted, I found a little cave in the rocks by the shore where nobody was, and fell asleep from sheer relief. But I awoke before dawn, feeling very cold, to find waves washing over me and reaching up to my head. It must have been low tide when I went in. No wonder the cave was empty.

I left the cave and started walking toward the hills.

Unlike Japan proper, where the rainy season begins in June, it comes a month earlier in Okinawa.

Naturally, being a child at the time, I knew nothing about seasons, but I was conscious of how bad the weather continued to be. May being the rainy season, and my clothes wringing-wet from my experience in the cave, the night wind made me very cold. My teeth chattered, and I was hungry. I found a vegetable patch and felt under the potato plants to see if I could dig up any sweet potatoes and sure enough I found some small leftover ones. Hurriedly shaking off the earth I crammed them into my mouth. I also found some carrots and ate them, too.

Feeling myself again, I set off once more along the broad stony road. Since it was not yet dawn, it was thronged with refugees. Suddenly, the sound of machine-gun fire coincided with a rain of bullets. A stone right by my feet was smashed to fragments that flew into my legs. I started to run frantically, but the bullets never stopped whistling past my ears.

Just then, I caught sight of a house on the left side of the road surrounded by a stone wall. I tumbled down beside the wall for protection and crawled along it to the house. The house was empty, but for some reason, of the crowds of people running screaming down the road, not one thought of hiding in the house. Many of them fell, hit by bullets.

I hid in the house until the group of refugees had gone by, thinking of how my father often cautioned me, "Tomiko, never just copy what other people do; always think things out for yourself." I remembered what I used to do when playing hide-and-seek: my secret was to avoid hiding near the others, for that was where the person who was "it" was bound to look. After that, I always made it a point to keep to myself as I fled.

The bullets finally stopped and everything became unbelievably quiet. I stayed in the house all day, and slept, and did not leave there until it was dark.

After walking a long time, I found myself on a wide road where I could see the sea on my left. I had no idea where I was. The road was muddy, and the canvas sports shoes I was wearing kept sticking in the mud. It was hard going as I picked my way, trying to avoid the worst places, and then right in front of me I saw a soldier lying in the road. Poor man, I thought, as I started to walk past him, he must have been killed by one of those bullets. By that time, I had seen so many dead bodies here and there that I had become quite used to the sight and was not frightened. But the soldier I thought was dead suddenly reached out his hand and grabbed hold of my ankle. As I let out a scream, he looked up at me with a grim expression and said, "Little girl, how's the war going?"

I thought for a moment, and then replied, "I think Japan's winning."

Whereupon, the terrible expression on his face gave way to a gentle smile.

"So we're winning. Thank you. Banzai!" he said in a rather hoarse voice, letting go of my ankle. Then his face fell forward into the mud and he did not look up again, nor did he move any more.

I did not really know whether we were winning or losing the war. I was simply doing as my father had taught me. "Tomiko," he had said, "it doesn't matter what you hear or who tells you, you mustn't ever say that Japan is losing, even if you're wrong." But even if my father had not told me to do so, I don't think I could have had the heart to let down a dying soldier with bad news. Although I was in a desperate situation myself, I still wanted to comfort him.

I am still haunted, after these many years, by the memory of that soldier, grasping my ankle with his muddy hand and being so braced by the thought of the Japanese Army's superiority and his belief in Japan's victory that he could summon up his last reserves of strength to cry out "Banzai!" with his dying breath.

As I wandered about searching for my sisters, I saw many a soldier still gripping his gun or his sword or his bayonet as he lay dead.

I had no idea at the time what day of the month it was, but judging by the records, I think it must have been somewhere between the end of May and the beginning of June 1945. We left our home in Shuri as refugees on the twelfth or thirteenth of May, and must have reached Makabe about the fourteenth or fifteenth. We stayed there for several days, so it was probably about the nineteenth or twentieth when we arrived at Komesu beach where our brother died. And it may have been anywhere from the twenty-first to the twenty-fourth that I was separated from my sisters. That would make it somewhere between the twenty-seventh and the thirty-first that I found myself on the road under machine-gun attack and took refuge in the empty house with the stone wall. American Army assault records show that from May 31 to June 4 an attack was made from Tomigusuku Village and Kochinda Town in the west to the Minato River in the east.

I think now that I was separated from my sisters

somewhere around Mabuni, east of Komesu beach, and the broad road where I encountered the machine-gun attack was the road to Tamagusuku Village, where I headed in the direction of Kochinda in my eagerness to press on. I was unwittingly going towards the action instead of away from it. This coincides with the American army records. I was, in fact, going northwards in a counterclockwise circle. Not a perfect circle, of course, since being only a little child not quite seven, who had no map or knowledge of geography, I simply zig-zagged around. That is why sometimes I would see the sea on my right and sometimes on my left. It seems certain that I was wandering around in the very center of the battle, which explains why I saw so many dead. Some days later, I came to a road I recognized. The four of us children had traveled together on this same road much earlier in our flight.

The Ants

I had made up my mind to avoid people as much as possible and chose roads without many refugees. I thus became quite used to traveling alone and was not even afraid at night. It was far more frightening in the daytime when we were perfect targets for the enemy behind us to bombard, shoot and strafe. So I always found a cave to hide in in the daytime and only came out at night to look for food and to continue walking.

One night it was cloudy and very dark. I had become accustomed to seeing in the dark and had no trouble at all walking at night. On moonlit nights I could see almost as well as in the daytime, and starry nights were pretty good, too. But that night there was not a single star to see by. Feeling with my hands, I searched around in a grassy area for a vegetable patch, but couldn't find one anywhere. I had apparently stumbled into an area with nothing but pampas grass.

Presently, my foot was aware of a slight depression. When you can't see with your eyes, your hands and feet have to take over and you develop a sort of animal sense. As I sat down and carefully felt ahead of me with my toes, my foot dropped right down and I slid into a hollow that came up as high as my chest. Before I knew it, I was asleep.

Next morning I found that the pampas grass growing all around made a sort of roof over my hole. When I climbed out of the hole and looked around, I was completely surrounded by pampas grass as tall as I was. I found a little mound and stood on it, and jumped up in the air a few times to see if I could see anything that resembled a vegetable field, but there was nothing but pampas grass as far as the eye could see.

My stomach was rumbling because I had had nothing to eat since the morning before. I felt weak with hunger, so I went back into the hollow and curled up, holding my tummy. That was when I saw something that looked like a thin black string, moving. I looked closer and saw it was a line of ants, and each one was carrying something white in its mouth. Why, there must be something to eat nearby! I thought. How funny, on a pampas moor.

I followed the ants for about five or six yards and all became clear. There lay a soldier, and near him was his haversack, black with ants. The soldier must have been dead for some time, as he had begun to decompose. His belly was swollen up like a balloon, and there was a terrible smell. Steeling myself, I opened the lid of the haversack, and what did I find inside but my favorite sugar drops! When I took them out there were just enough to cover my palm. I put my hands together, as if to pray, and said softly, "Mr. Soldier, may I have these sweets? You're dead, so you won't be able to eat them." I gazed at the sugar drops for awhile, then I put two or three down for the ants. After that I said *"Itadakimasu,"* which means "I gratefully partake," a sort of grace we always say in Japan before eating. Then I put one of the sugar drops in my mouth and bit it. It was lovely and crunchy, and filled my mouth with sweetness.

That handful of candy pepped me up enormously. "Thank you, Mr. Soldier, thank you, ants" I said to myself. Henceforth, I always felt that dead soldiers were my friends, providing me with things to eat, and was no longer afraid of them, but I really was afraid of live soldiers. Those soldiers at Komesu beach had hardly allowed us any time at all to mourn our dear brother. I became skillful in deciding whether a soldier was alive or dead. Whenever I found one lying on the ground, I made quite sure first, from a distance, before running over to him. If a soldier did not react at all to the sound of a bomb or a shell, then he was dead and it was safe to approach him. If he moved a hand or leg or any part of his body at the sound of a bomb bursting, he was still alive. Once, though, I made a dreadful mistake.

I was quite sure the soldier was dead and after folding my hands politely in prayer, I had stretched out my hand to partake of what was in his haversack, when I felt a large hand on my shoulder. Letting out a little scream I said, "Oh, I am sorry" and fell over backwards. I was so frightened I couldn't move for some time, and just lay there trembling. But in spite of it all, I was so hungry that I went back and put my hand in his haversack. There were sugar drops, hard biscuits, and a can of salmon.

I managed to make a small hole in the lid of the can by pressing it hard against a pointed stone. But the stone became blunt in the process, so I found another stone and made the hole a little bigger. When the hole was big enough, I managed to get the contents out by using two twigs like chopsticks. As far as I remember I had never been shown how to open a can, but somehow, extreme hunger taught me what to do.

The reason the pampas moor I had strayed into was completely devoid of people was that you could see right into it from the air; it was no good as a hiding place. There was nobody there but me, the dead soldier, and some small animals that had taken refuge from the noise of the bombing and shelling. A goat, startled by a bomb, tore right past me through the pampas grass, and I could see American planes over the valley dropping bombs, soon followed by terrific explosions that rocked the ground.

The Rat's Gift

It was now broad daylight and I thought I might become a target, so I looked around frantically for a hole to hide in. But no matter how I searched among the pampas grass, there was not a hole to be found anywhere. Then I remembered that my father had once said, "If you are fated to die, it doesn't matter where you go, you're bound to die. And if you're meant to live, you'll survive all sorts of dangers." So I gave up my frantic search. I decided that if I was going to die anyway, I might as well enjoy myself as much as possible, and that it would be better to die in the fresh air than in one of those smelly caves. And besides, what was the use of finding a cave that was so full of people already that they drove you away? After all, I had got into the habit of avoiding people and keeping to myself.

And yet, I didn't like the idea of dying there in the pampas moor like that soldier and becoming a weather-beaten skeleton. Wondering where it would be best to die, I made up my mind to find a hole of my own after all. A small one would do.

After searching for a long time, I finally found a small opening in the ground. But even as I prepared to die, food became the next priority. I had eaten all the food that belonged to the soldier and no matter how I searched I could not find so much as the tail end of a sweet potato. I wondered if I would die in this hole, and the thought that nobody would ever find me suddenly filled me with sadness. I thought of my strict father and my sweet mother, and my sisters Yoshiko and Hatsuko who went so far as to slap my cheek in their anxiety that I should eat my rice, and Nini, who always used to play with me. One by one their faces passed before me in my mind. How nice and warm my father's broad back had felt when he carried me piggyback! And my mother's lovely lullabies! The thought of my parents gave me a moment or two of calm.

It was just then that I saw a rat carrying a small sweet potato in its front paws. When it saw me, it was so startled it dropped the sweet potato and scuttled away. I was startled too, but I was so hungry I picked up the sweet potato, saying, "Oh, you nice mousie!" and after scraping off the rat's tooth-marks on a nearby stone I sank my teeth ravenously into it.

"Thank you, Mr. Rat," I said, when I had gobbled it up. Not only was I grateful to him for the sweet potato, but for his letting me know that there was a vegetable plot nearby.

Once again I was filled with the courage to go on living. I must find that vegetable plot, I said to myself, then I can eat some more sweet potatoes!

Nini the Rabbit

I set off the next day, but no matter where I went, the pampas moor just stretched on endlessly, with nothing even remotely resembling a field of vegetables. It began to rain, and I knew I would soon become drenched if I didn't find another cave.

Then, ahead of me, I saw a clump of pampas that was taller than the rest, and down by its roots was a hole. Thank goodness, I thought, and slid into it, landing on my backside with a thud. As I did so, I felt something warm under me. Oh dear, I said to myself, I've sat down on a dying soldier! I lifted my bottom ever so gingerly and peeked.

It was a white rabbit!

Maybe it was someone's lost pet rabbit? It was looking up at me with its crimson eyes, twitching its whiskers, wriggling its nose, and trembling. It seemed terrified by the continual noise of exploding bombs and shells, for it made no attempt to run away when I appeared.

"Sorry to come in suddenly like that. I must have hurt you," I said, stroking its back. The rabbit laid back its long ears and blinked. Every time a bomb burst it flinched, and gave a shudder.

"It's all right. Those bombs are bursting over in

the valley. That one was a long way off."

I held the rabbit in my arms and spoke to it every time there was an explosion. Talking to it made me feel better too. The rabbit felt so nice and soft and warm in my arms. After awhile, the rabbit stopped trembling.

"There now, that's better isn't it? You must have been awfully scared. Let's go to sleep together now, like this, okay?"

Of course the rabbit didn't answer, but it was wonderful to have someone to talk to once more. I soon began to feel drowsy and before I knew it I was fast asleep.

I dreamed about Nini, my brother who died at Komesu. He was holding my hand and wanting me to go somewhere to play. On the way we came to a rushing stream and I was afraid to cross it, and cried. But Nini held my hand tightly and said, "It's all right, Tomiko. I'm here with you. Just be brave and we'll cross together," and he put his arm around me and got me safely to the other side. Then we came to a large meadow covered with yellow mustard flowers, and I was so happy I shrieked with joy as we played about. Then it began to get dark, and Nini said, "Mommy will be worried, so we'd better be going home."

"I don't want to go yet," I demurred, "I'm thirsty. I want a drink of water."

"Oh, shucks. Well, all right. Try this. You eat it this way," said Nini, and picked a stalk of bamboo or pampas—I don't know what it was exactly—some kind of edible plant that grew nearby, and showed me how to munch it.

"The juice is sweet. Try it."

I ate the piece he handed me, but it didn't have any

taste at all. Then the scene changed and we were on the road home and came to that rushing stream once more.

"Give me your hand, Tomiko. Now, hold on tightly to mine."

I clutched Nini's hand for all I was worth, when suddenly the current became stronger and my feet felt as if they would be carried away. I screamed, "Nini, I'm scared!"

My own scream woke me up. I was clutching the rabbit's forelegs with all my strength, and its head was wet with my tears.

It occurred to me then that Mother had felt sorry for me in my lonesome state and had sent Nini to me in the guise of the rabbit. Yes! That was it.

I had no idea how long I had been in that hole. I peeked outside and found the rain had cleared completely, and the moon was shining.

I decided to call the rabbit Nini. Neither of us had anything to eat, so I thought I would pick some grass for him, and there in among the pampas near our hole I suddenly noticed a weed that looked exactly like the kind that my brother had shown me how to eat in my dream. I crawled out and picked some and put it in my mouth, and lo and behold, I found my mouth filled with a sweet juice!

It was fantastic. Just as my brother Nini had said in my dream, the leaves of the weed were delicious. I picked some of the tenderest-looking leaves for Nini the rabbit, who munched them with gusto.

"Let's stick it out together, Nini, to the end," I said. "We can live on this. And we don't need swords or guns to protect ourselves with. After all, theirs didn't protect those soldiers from being killed." I had seen more dead soldiers than I could count.

Nini gazed up at my mouth as I ate. He was probably trying to tell me that he wanted something more to eat. But to me it seemed as if he were my dead brother saying, "That's right, Tomiko, you eat that grass and stay alive."

Nini Saves My Life

I made up my mind I would find some carrots for Nini. I wanted to take Nini with me, but being white, I was afraid he would be too conspicuous in the moonlight. And besides, it would have been too cruel if he were killed a second time, having already died once at Komesu.

"Wait for me here, Nini," I said. "I'm going to find you some nice carrots. Be good, now, and don't go out."

I put Nini the rabbit as far back as possible in the hole and stuffed the entrance with pampas grass, and then I tied some stalks of pampas together as a landmark, so I could find the place when I came back.

I had not gone very far when I saw in the distance what looked like a field. As I made my way through the pampas, I kept repeating over and over to myself the words "Carrots, carrots," as if they were a magic formula. The pampas grass suddenly gave way, and there was the field.

But what should I see right in the middle of the field but a human-like figure. It was white, and swaying around. A ghost, I thought, and dropped to the ground. But then, looking carefully, I saw that what I thought was a ghost was the top half of man clad in the sort of white cotton undershirt soldiers wear. He was bending forward, writhing in agony. When I looked closer to see why he was doing so, I saw that he was cutting his own belly with a short sword, but he had not yet died and was in great pain. I could hear him groaning. And then I noticed another soldier holding a long Japanese sword. He went behind the writhing, swaying soldier and put his hands together and prayed, then he moved to one side and I saw the blade of his sword flash in the light of the moon.

Suddenly, I was terrified, and turned and ran as fast as my legs would carry me. I didn't want to risk being discovered.

I had no idea what was going on. It was not until years later that I understood that one of the soldiers had been committing hara-kiri and the other assisting him by cutting off his head to put him out of his misery. At the time, I was startled, and very frightened.

I found another field, where I dug up some carrots and hurried back with them to the hole where Nini was. But the hole was empty. Where could he be? And here I had brought him his favorite carrots. I was suddenly very upset. Could he by chance have followed me? I retraced my path back through the pampas, softly calling, "Nini! Nini!"

But although I went all the way back to the field where I had dug up the carrots, I could find no sign of Nini. Just then, there was a terrific explosion behind me. I turned around and saw that the entire area around the hole where Nini and I had found solace had turned bright red. The pampas grass was a sea of flames. An incendiary bomb had landed right by our hole. The object of an incendiary bomb is to destroy buildings and vegetation, so it is made to burn everything within a fixed radius with a very intense heat.

If Nini had been there in the hole when I got back, and if I hadn't gone out to look for him, I would have perished in that inferno. Animals are said to have a sixth sense that warns them of danger. I believed Nini's premonition of the incendiary bomb had saved my life. I was profoundly grateful to Nini. But at the same time, I felt terribly sad to have lost my dear little companion. "I hope you're alive somewhere and that you're all right, Nini," I said, leaving one of the carrots for him in the hope that he would find it if he was still alive. And I said a little prayer.

Staying Alive

by David Wagoner

*This poem advises you how to stay alive if
you are alone and lost in the woods. What
might Karana think of this advice?*

Staying alive in the woods is a matter of calming down
At first and deciding whether to wait for rescue,
Trusting to others,
Or simply to start walking and walking in one direction
5 Till you come out—or something happens to stop you.
By far the safer choice
Is to settle down where you are, and try to make a
    living
Off the land, camping near water, away from shadows.
Eat no white berries;
10 Spit out all bitterness. Shooting at anything
Means hiking further and further every day
To hunt survivors;
It may be best to learn what you have to learn without
    a gun,
Not killing but watching birds and animals go
15 In and out of shelter
At will. Following their example, build for a whole
    season:
Facing across the wind in your lean-to,
You may feel wilder,
But nothing, not even you, will have to stay in hiding.
20 If you have no matches, a stick and a fire-bow
Will keep you warmer,
Or the crystal of your watch, filled with water, held up
    to the sun
Will do the same in time. In case of snow
Drifting toward winter,
25 Don't try to stay awake through the night, afraid of
    freezing—
The bottom of your mind knows all about zero;

It will turn you over
And shake you till you waken. If you have trouble
    sleeping
Even in the best of weather, jumping to follow
30 With eyes strained to their corners
The unidentifiable noises of the night and feeling
Bears and packs of wolves nuzzling your elbow,
Remember the trappers
Who treated them indifferently and were left alone.

35 If you hurt yourself, no one will comfort you
Or take your temperature,
So stumbling, wading, and climbing are as dangerous as
    flying.
But if you decide, at last, you must break through
In spite of all danger,

40 Think of yourself by time and not by distance, counting
Wherever you're going by how long it takes you;
No other measure
Will bring you safe to nightfall. Follow no streams: they
    run
Under the ground or fall into wilder country.

45 Remember the stars
And moss when your mind runs into circles. If it should
    rain
Or the fog should roll the horizon in around you,
Hold still for hours
Or days if you must, or weeks, for seeing is believing

50 In the wilderness. And if you find a pathway,
Wheel-rut, or fence-wire,
Retrace it left or right: someone knew where he was
    going
Once upon a time, and you can follow
Hopefully, somewhere,

55 Just in case. There may even come, on some uncanny
    evening,
A time when you're warm and dry, well fed, not thirsty,
Uninjured, without fear,
When nothing, either good or bad, is happening.
This is called staying alive. It's temporary.

60 What occurs after
Is doubtful. You must always be ready for something to
    come bursting

Through the far edge of a clearing, running toward you,
Grinning from ear to ear
And hoarse with welcome. Or something crossing and
    hovering
65   Overhead, as light as air, like a break in the sky,
Wondering what you are.
Here you are face to face with the problem of
    recognition.
Having no time to make smoke, too much to say,
You should have a mirror
70   With a tiny hole in the back for better aiming, for
    reflecting
Whatever disaster you can think of, to show
The way you suffer.
These body signals have universal meaning: If you are
    lying
Flat on your back with arms outstretched behind you,
75   You say you require
Emergency treatment; if you are standing erect and
    holding
Arms horizontal, you mean you are not ready;
If you hold them over
Your head, you want to be picked up. Three of
    anything
80   Is a sign of distress. Afterward, if you see
No ropes, no ladders,
No maps or messages falling, no searchlights or trails
    blazing,
Then, chances are, you should be prepared to burrow
Deep for a deep winter.

Change

by Charlotte Zolotow

*As season after season passed on her
island, Karana may have felt the way the
speaker in this poem does.*

The summer
still hangs
heavy and sweet
with sunlight
5 as it did last year.

The autumn
still comes
showering gold and crimson
as it did last year.

10 The winter
still stings
clean and cold and white
as it did last year.

The spring
15 still comes
like a whisper in the dark night.

It is only I
who have changed.

Acknowledgments

Continued from page ii

David Wagoner: "Staying Alive," from *Collected Poems, 1956–1976* by David Wagoner. Copyright © 1976 by David Wagoner. Reprinted by permission of the author.

Scott Treimel New York: "Change," from *River Winding* by Charlotte Zolotow. Copyright © 1970 by Charlotte Zolotow. Reprinted by permission of Scott Treimel New York for the author.